For Barbara
An enthusiasm we share.

Affectionately

Paul

TENDRIL
a poetry magazine

Tendril Magazine Presents:

the Poet's Choice

Edited by George E. Murphy, Jr.

Associate Editors: Moira Linehan
Chuck Ozug

Cover Photograph by Mel Goldman
   Mel Goldman Studios, 329 Newbury Street, Boston

Composition, layout, and design by George E. Murphy Jr.
   Wampeter Composition, Box 512, Green Harbor, Mass. 02041

"To A Troubled Friend" copyright ©1957 by James Wright.
Reprinted from Collected Poems by permission of Wesleyan University Press.

The publication of this special issue of *Tendril* magazine is supported by grants from the Coordinating Council of Literary Magazines and The Massachusetts Council on the Arts & Humanities.

Subscribers to *Tendril* will receive *The Poet's Choice* as issue No. 9.

First Edition.

Copyright © 1980 by *Tendril, Inc.*
                    P.O. Box 512, Green Harbor, Massachusetts 02041

Printed in the U.S.A.

Library of Congress Catalog Card Number: 80-52566
ISBN: 0-937504-00-9
ISSN: 0197-890X

Tendril Magazine, Inc. is directed and alternately edited by Moira Linehan, George E. Murphy Jr., and Chuck Ozug. *Tendril* is published three times per year in January, May, and September. Single issues are $3. Individual subscriptions are $6 for 3 issues. Institutional subscriptions are $8 for 3 issues.

Tendril, Inc. is a non-profit, tax-exempt organization dedicated to publishing poetry that is "concise, imagistic, and evocative." All contributions to *Tendril* are tax-deductable. All Patrons making a gift to *Tendril* of $100 or more will receive a free lifetime subscription.

Tendril is indexed in the *Index of American Periodical Verse.*

Acknowledgements

Ai: "Pentecost" is reprinted from the book THE KILLING FLOOR by Ai published by Houghton Mifflin Company, Boston. Copyright © 1979 by Ai.

A.R. Ammons: "Room Conditioner" first appeared in *Tendril* and is reprinted by permission of the author.

Philip Appleman: "Memo To the 21st Century" first appeared in the *Chicago Tribune Sunday Magazine* and is reprinted from OPEN DOORWAYS (Norton, 1976) by permission of the author.

Amiri Baraka:"Reprise of one of A.G.'s Best Poems!" Copyright © 1979 by Amiri Baraka, reprinted from SELECTED POEMS by permission of William Morrow & Co.

Marvin Bell: "He Said To" first appeared in *Water Table* and is reprinted by permission of the author.

Suzanne E. Berger: "Mornings" is reprinted from THESE ROOMS (Penmaen Press, 1979) by permission of the author.

Robert Bly: "The Fallen Tree" Copyright © 1979 by Robert Bly, From the book THIS TREE WILL BE HERE FOR A THOUSAND YEARS. Reprinted by permission of Harper & Row Publishers, Inc.

Philip Booth: "Eaton's Boatyard" first appeared in *American Poetry Review* and is reprinted by permission of the author.

Olga Broumas: "Absence Of Noise   Presence Of Sound" is reprinted from SOIE SAUVAGE (Copper Canyon Press, 1979) by permission of the author.

Charles Bukowski: "A Love Poem For All The Women I Have Known" first appeared in *Wormwood Review* and is reprinted by permission of the author.

Hayden Carruth: "Contra Mortem" © 1966 by Hayden Carruth. Courtesy of Author and Publisher. Reprinted by permission of New Directions Publishing Corporation.

Ray Carver: "Luck" first appeared in *Kayak 50*, May 1979 and is reprinted by permission of the author.

Philip Dacey: "Form Rejection Letter" first appeared in *Shenandoah* and is reprinted by permission of the author.

Madeline DeFrees: "First Class Relics: Letter To Dennis Finnell" appears by permission of the author.

Stephen Dobyns: "The Delicate Plummeting Bodies" is reprinted by permission; © 1980 *The New Yorker* Magazine, Inc.

Norman Dubie: "The Pennacesse Leper Colony For Women. Cape Cod. 1922." is reprinted from IN THE DEAD OF THE NIGHT by Norman Dubie by permission of the University of Pittsburgh Press. © 1975 by University of Pittsburgh Press.

Richard Eberhart: "To Alpha Dryden Eberhart November 26, 1977, on being seventy-five" is reprinted from WONDERS: WRITINGS FOR THE CHILDREN IN ALL OF US (Summit/Rolling Stone Press Books, 1980) by permission of the author.

Russell Edson: "Pigeons" is reprinted from WITH SINCEREST REGARDS (Burning Deck, 1980) by permission of the author.

Alan Feldman: "Personals" copyright © 1980 is printed by permission of the author.

Carolyn Forché: "Reunion" is reprinted from *American Poetry Review* by permission of the author.

Tess Gallagher: "Bird-Window-Flying" by Tess Gallagher is reprinted by permission, © 1979, *The New Yorker* Magazine, Inc.

Brendan Galvin: "The Old Trip By Dream Train" first appeared in *Georgia Review* and is reprinted from ATLANTIC FLYWAY (University of Georgia Press, 1980) by permission of the author.

Gary Gildner: "Today They Are Roasting Rocky Norse" first appeared in *New Letters* and is reprinted from THE RUNNER by Gary Gildner (University of Pittsburgh Press, 1978) by permission of the author.

Louise Glück: "Lamentations" copyright © 1980 by Louise Gluck first appeared in *The New Republic* and is reprinted from DESCENDING FIGURE (Ecco, 1980) by permission of the publisher and the author.

Linda Gregg: "The Defeated" first appeared in *Ironwood* and is reprinted from TOO BRIGHT TO SEE (Greywolf Press, 1980) by permission of the author.

Marilyn Hacker: "La Fontaine De Vaucluse" first appeared in *MS.* and is reprinted by permission of the author.

John Haines: "Deserted Cabin" copyright © 1966 by John Haines. Reprinted from WINTER NEWS (Wesleyan University Press, 1966) by permission of Wesleyan University Press.

Donald Hall: "Ox Cart Man" by Donald Hall is reprinted by permission; © 1977 *The New Yorker* Magazine, Inc. and from KICKING THE LEAVES (Harper & Row, 1978) by permission of the author.

Mark Strand: "Elegy For My Father" is reprinted from THE STORY OF OUR LIVES by
   Mark Strand. Copyright © 1973by Mark Strand. Used by permission of Atheneum
   Publishers.
Lucien Stryk: "Cherries" first appeared in *Poetry* June 1978. Copyright © 1978 by the
   Modern Poetry Association and is reprinted by permission of the editor of *Poetry*.
Dabney Stuart: "The Opposite Field" first appeared in *Tendril* and is reprinted by per-
   mission of the author.
David Swanger: "Rowing In Turns" is printed by permission of the author.
James Tate: "Nobody's Business' first appeared in the *Massachusetts Review* and is re-
   printed by permission of the author.
Phyllis Thompson:"Eurydice" first appeared in *Hudson Review* and is reprinted by per-
   mission of the author.
John Unterecker: "Portrait" first appeared in *Kayak* 48, June 1978 in a slightly different
   form and is reprinted by permission of the author.
David Wagoner: "Under The Sign Of The Moth" first appeared in *Poetry* January 1980.
   Copyright © 1980 by the Modern Poetry Association and is reprinted by per-
   mission of the editor of *Poetry*.
Diane Wakoski: "My Mother's Milkman" first appeared in *Louisville Review* and is reprin-
   ted from CAP OF DARKNESS (Black Sparrow, 1980) by permission of the
   author.
Cary Waterman: "Love Poem" is reprinted from THE SALAMANDER MIGRATION
   (University of Pittsburgh Press, 1980) by permission of the University of Pitts-
   burgh Press. Copyright © 1980 by Cary Waterman.
Theodore Weiss: "En Route" first appeared in *The New Republic* and is reprinted by per-
   mission of the author.
Richard Wilbur: "Transit" by Richard Wilbur is reprinted by permission; © 1979, *The New
   Yorker* Magazine,Inc.
Charles Wright: "Called Back" first appeared in *Paris Review* and is reprinted by permission
   of the author.
Paul Zweig: "A Fly On The Water" first appeared in *American Poetry Review* and is reprinted
   by permission of the author.

The editors would also like to acknowledge the encouragement, assistance, and advice
of The Avenue Victor Hugo Bookstore, Mel Goldman, Steve Gordon, Mary Harrington,
Rosemary Murphy, Herbert Rogalski, and Louisa Solano of the Grolier Bookstore.

Dedicated to the Memory of James Wright

1927-1980

To A Troubled Friend

Weep, and weep long, but do not weep for me,
Nor, long lamenting, raise, for any word
Of mine that beats above you like a bird,
Your voice, or hand. But shaken clear, and free,
Be the bare maple, bough where nests are made
Snug in the season's wrinkled cloth of frost;
Be leaf, by hardwood knots, by tendrils crossed
On tendrils, stripped, uncaring; give no shade.

Give winter nothing; hold; and let the flake
Poise or dissolve along your upheld arms.
All flawless hexagons may melt and break;
While you must feel the summer's rage of fire,
Beyond this frigid season's empty storms,
Banished to bloom, and bear the bird's desire.

CONTENTS

INTRODUCTION

In The Passionate Perils of Publishing (Booklegger Press, 1978), Celeste West presents a rather grim view of the present trend in the publishing world toward the conglomerate takeover of publishing houses:

"... the folks who bring us twinkies (ITT); panty hose, ci-gars and films (Gulf & Western); financial services (Dun & Bradstreet); vacuum cleaners (Scott & Fetzer); and military hardware (Raytheon, RCA, Litton, ITT, IBM) also control much of what we're offered to read ...eight houses [Ran-dom House, Knopf, Ballantine Books, Modern Library, Vintage, Pantheon, L.W. Singer, and Beginner Books] are the different publishing imprints owned by RCA, the six billion dollar a year conglomerate. A huge defense contrac-tor, RCA also owns NBC tv and radio stations, and markets more then 60,000 products - from Hertz Rent-A-Cars, Ban-quet Foods and Coronet Rugs to records and electronic equipment."

In the three year period of 1975-1977, there were over 160 mergers of major publishing houses. Even the House Judiciary Subcommittee on Mono-polies as well as the Senate Antitrust and Monopoly Subcommittee are current-ly investigating conglomerate takeovers in publishing.

With the high financing available to such conglomerates, the media can be so effectively used that best-sellers can be effectively guaranteed - budgeted, designed, and *made* to sell. Anyone interested in the future of literature should look closely at such successes as Jaws II, a team-contracted, written-to-order novel based on a film-script based, in turn, on an extraneous idea about an aqua-tic non-character which appeared in a book by Peter Benchley -- certainly more of a media event than a work of literature. As more and more publishing houses are taken over by conglomerates disinterested in literature per se, it is easy to understand how high profits, based on careful and extensive market research, become the primary criterion of value in what is chosen for publication. While it is not necessarily true that conglomerate ownership results in editorial mal-feasance (RCA-owned Knopf and Random House, for example, continue to be active in literary publishing), the thrust toward maximum profit vs. minimal risks and losses most certainly curtails receptivity towards first novels and, of course, poetry. Recently a number of publishing houses have publicly forsworn poetry and fiction in favor of more profitable gothic romances and how-to books.

Should the argument for artistic compromise seem inflated on our part, take a minute to notice the prior publication sources of the 100 poems collected here. With few exceptions, they were published not by major publishing houses but by non-profit university or small presses and magazines which have become the care-takers and promoters of most of the literature now being written in America.

Eighteen years ago, Time magazine reported that, "In a country where on-ly half the adults read even one book of any kind a year, the poet is virtually ig-nored." In 1980, the statistic more commonly cited to reflect that portion of the population that reads is only 15%. But the poet is no longer ignored. In this era of conglomerate merger, perhaps because of it, poetry is enjoying a resur-gence in popularity. Last January, 500 poets and friends of poetry were guests at a White House reception. Poetry readings around the country are often given to standing-room-only crowds. Though the merits of the movement are often questioned, there is a grass-roots renaissance taking place; new cost-shaving developments in print technology coupled with the inability of too many good writers to find publishers have led to the start of thousands of small, independent presses and magazines. The trends are likely to continue and it seems only a matter of time before the literate American public becomes aware of the need to support and subscribe to the efforts of these independent publishers whose motivation has more to do with love than money.

Tendril magazine is part of this movement. In 1977, Mark Cohen, John Hennelly, Moira Linehan, Chuck Ozug, and myself pooled our money and, with some further financial help from a friend, Steve Baisden, began publishing because we love poetry. Through faith, hard work, the good-will of writers and friends, and recently some financial assistance , *Tendril* has survived the difficult beginnings of such a venture. Now, three years later, with this 9th issue, our most ambitious project, we hope to reach a new, wider audience, to make some inroads into the biggest problem facing all small publishers -distribution - and to achieve something resembling temporary financial security so that we can devote less time to survival tactics and more time to the pleasures and perils of publishing the work of serious and deserving writers that might otherwise remain unpublished.

As for <u>The Poet's Choice</u>, the concept for the anthology, once articulated, seemed marvelously *right,* a simple and interesting idea. We all had favorite poems from the work of the poets we admired. But what, we wondered, would be *their* choice as favorite?

To begin, the editors compiled lists of 100 poets. In such a limited framework, we assumed from the outset that it would be inevitable that we would overlook many distinguished poets but *our* choice was to indulge our own various editorial preferences and biases. We decided to pay no attention whatsoever to race, sex, geography, or politics. We also refrained from asking for any explanation for the choice. Since such a choice might be made on aesthetic, critical, sentimental, or intuitive grounds, we were afraid that the need to "justify" or explain the choice might inhibit the choosing process. We also felt that the poems should speak for themselves. Then we mailed our invitations and waited.

Some invitations, we found out later, were lost in the mail. A few poets declined; some found choosing impossible. But to our great satisfaction, 100 poets rose to the task of making that choice, of committing themselves, at least for the moment, to a "favorite" poem. Here they are, presented without comment, arranged alphabetically by author.

An artist, of course, is not always the best critic of his or her art and the poems collected here may or may not reflect the best of each poet's work. But, whether we agree with the poet's choice or not, the collection offers a unique insight: each choice can serve to inform the reader of that poet's personal vision as well as present us with a sampling of what he or she considers to be some fulfillment of that vision. In that sense, I believe this is a remarkable anthology, rich in its diversity, a wealth of intelligent and vivid work by 100 of our best living poets. Enjoy.

George E. Murphy, Jr.
Ocean Bluff, Massachusetts
7/7/80

Ai

Pentecost

For Myself

Rosebud Morales, my friend,
before you deserted,
you'd say anyone can kill an Indian
and forget it the same instant,
that it will happen to me, Emiliano Zapata.
But my men want more corn for tortillas,
more pigs, more chickens, more chilis
and land.
If I haven't got a gun or a knife,
I'll fight with a pitchfork or a hoe,
to take them from the bosses,
those high-flying birds,
with the pomade glistening on their hair,
as they promenade into their coffins.
And if I'm killed, if we're all killed right now,
we'll go on, the true Annunciation.

Rosebud, how beautiful this day is.
I'm riding to meet Guajardo.
He'll fight with me now,
against Carranza.
When I get to the hacienda, it's quiet.
Not many soldiers,
a sorrel horse, its reins held
by a woman in a thin, white American dress
and Guajardo standing on a balcony.

I get off my horse and start up the steps.
My legs burn, my chest,
my jaw, my head.
There's a hill in front of me;
it's slippery, I have to use my hands to climb it.
At the top, it's raining fire and blood
on rows and rows of black corn.
Machetes are scattered everywhere.
I grab one and start cutting the stalks.
When they hit the ground,
they turn into men.
I yell at them.
You're damned in the cradle,
in the grave, even in Heaven.
Dying doesn't end anything.
Get up. Swing those machetes.
You can't steal a man's glory
without a goddamned fight.
Boys, take the land, take it; it's yours.
If you suffer in the grave,
you can kill from it.

A.R. Ammons

Room Conditioner

After rain I
walk and looking
down glimpse
the moon: I
back up to see
and the mere
puddle splices
on to two hundred
thousand miles of
height two
hundred thousand
miles of depth.

Philip Appleman

Memo to the 21st Century

It was like this once: sprinklers mixed
our marigolds with someone else's phlox,
and the sidewalks under maple trees
were lacy with August shade,
and whistles called at eight and fathers walked
to work, and when they blew again,
men in tired blue shirts followed
their shadows home to grass.
That is how it was in Indiana.

Towns fingered out to country once,
where brown-eyed daisies waved a fringe on orchards
and cattle munched at clover, and
fishermen sat in rowboats and were silent,
and on gravel roads, boys and girls
stopped their cars and felt the moon and touched,
and the quiet moments ringed and focused
lakes   moon   flowers.
That is how it was
in Indiana.

But we are moving out now,
scraping the world smooth where apples blossomed,
paving it over for cars. In the spring
before the clover goes purple,
we mean to scrape the hayfield, and
next year the hickory woods:
we are pushing on, our giant diesels snarling,
and I think of you, the billions of you, wrapped
in your twenty-first century concrete,
and I want to call to you, to let you know
that if you dig down,
down past wires and pipes
and sewers and subways, you will find
a crumbly stuff called earth. Listen:
in Indiana once, things grew in it.

Amiri Baraka

Reprise of one of A.G.'s Best Poems!

America existed in
               its ribboned
               columns
               in its matrix
               of screams
                  & pioneers

               (to the end!
               to the max!

               America existed
               in its own memory
               as its own vanity
               a butcher in a cowboy suit

               in its columbus' myths
               told by Flip Wilson
               they sd, "flip
                    flip
                       flip"

                  ac-dc
                in the dark
                teeth glowed green

               America had money belts that
                 glowed green in the
                     dark like Flip
                         Wilson's teeth

               Flip Wilson's teeth were gold
                   pharoahs hung around
                       Jesse Jackson's neck

               a pioneer of the late 20th century
                   inspiring Morgan think tanks to new creativity
                   on ways to trick bloods

                  Peanut jesus Jimmy riding niggers like ashy rolls royces

               America Warhol
               America Starsky
               America rhythm hats thrown up
             & they bleed from straw murders, stingy murders, homburg murders
               tyrolean, snapbrim
               & cowboy hat murders

America an imperialist bandit bleeding out the bowels
       wipe its ass w/ a dollar bill
       wipe its ass w/ a Latino peasant
       wipe its ass w/ yo' mamma you let it

    In its bicentennial jism
    In its death penalty enema
    America
    Allen Ginsberg sd
    "Go fuck yrself w/ yr
    Atom Bomb"   ----and yr doing
                    it!!

    He is one of yr prophets
        blind and crazy
        a metaphysical
        petty bourgeois
        intellectual
        "strummin & hummin
        all day"
            the image of the
            happy
            slave

We wade in the water
                America
                America
We wade in the bleeding
We wade in the screaming
       in the unemployment
       in the frustrated wives
       & impotent husbands
       of the dying middle
       class,
       in the middle of its
       workers
       its niggers
       its wild intelligent
       spics
       its
       brutalized
       chicanos
       its women out of work, again

Hymn poem for the passing into
       for the change into
            the transformation

America
>>yr going Communist
>>yr bourgeoisie oppose it
>>& their sell out lackie
>>fools
>>but yr going communist
>>>>America

>>>>Maybe you need to be
>>>>investigated
>>>>>>for yr unamerican
>>>>>>activities

>>>Yr shielding
>>>Commies

>>>I'm a red pinko Commie
>>>>A Communist
>>>>A Marxist-Leninist
>>>>>Whose ideology is
>>>>>>Marxism-Leninism-Mao Tse Tung Thought!

America, Communism is the only way
>>>for you
>the only way
>>>for the world
Capitalism
>>is dying
& its killing, has killed,
>>too many
>>already.

Private property is a metaphysical concept
the land, the wealth, belongs
to the people
"Better Red, let a small group of others,
be Dead"

I'm going to stop calling you, "America"
>Yr the United Snakes -- alright
>>>>>>United States
>A.G. thought you was "America"
>>because that was your myth-name
>>>yr promise
>>>>yr Golden
>>>>>name,

              yr name of
                  collectivity
                      & Communism

But the rest of us know yr the U.S.A.
          the United States
              of America
          The Capitalists' Shangri-La

Explosion is yr middle and "maiden"
name. Violence
 yr mid-wife.
          Explosion will birth you into
              Change
                  Dont think the Rebellion 60's
                  got you over. The poverty pimp
                  Frankensteins & Jack-Leg Politicians
                  will not stop the flow of "is"!

You got to do it
          & go through
              it

      Yeh - even you, America - got to change
          even you, America - got to change

      America - merica merica
          merica merica merica
          merii - caaaaaaa
      run the world to yr
      rich folks
      to the swine perverts
      who run you
      & if they tell you, "Over they dead bodies"
                      tell them
                      its the only
                      way!

Marvin Bell

He Said To

crawl *toward* the machine guns
except to freeze
for explosions and flares.
It was still ninety degrees
at night in North Carolina,
August, rain and all.
The tracer bullets **wanted**
our asses, which we swore to keep
down, and the highlight
of this preposterous exercise
was finding myself in mud
and water during flares. I
hurried in the darkness --
over things and under things --
to reach the next black pool
in time, and once
I lay in the cool salve that
so suited all I had become
for two light-ups of the sky.
I took one inside and one
face of two watches I ruined
doing things like that,
and made a watch that works.
From the combat
infiltration course and
common sense, I made a man
to survive the Army, which means
that I made a man to survive
being a man.

Suzanne E. Berger

Mornings

Quiet until now,
that moment like a startled bird
darts between us at our meal:
It was in the morning,
you stood at the counter,
looking at the snow.
Father came up behind you,
and cupped your breasts,
and held them for a long time.
I stood in the doorway, watching.

That Saturday morning was newborn
in the mother-and-father light:
your breasts like pears
that never really shaped
until I watched him shine them.
Look how we always shelve our breasts,
indelicately, on top of tables.

Yesterday, in the long mirror,
I surveyed the thickened waist
I haven't earned, as you did.
Hands on hips, alert to rustlings
on my small estate,
I heard nothing but silence.
I saw only ribbons leftover from Christmas,
the cat flung like a shawl on the blanket,
an old tulip of dark blood
on my twice-washed sheets:
I said aloud to my rooms,
In my house will it always be this quiet?

Years from now, perhaps,
I will come to this same table,
and ask an unborn daughter:
Tell me about the time
you saw him cup my breasts with tender hands,
and how you stayed for a long time,
that morning,
standing in the doorway, watching.

Robert Bly

The Fallen Tree

After a long walk I come down to the shore.
A cottonwood tree lies stretched out in the grass.
This tree knocked down by lightning —
and a hollow the owls made open now to the rain.
Disasters are all right, if they teach
      men and women
to turn their hollow places up.

The tree lies stretched out
      where it fell on the grass.
It is so mysterious, waters below, waters above,
so little of it we can ever know!

Philip Booth

Eaton's Boatyard

To make do, making a living:
                     to throw away nothing,
practically nothing, nothing that may
come in handy:
                  within an inertia of caked paintcans,
frozen C-clamps, blown strips of tarp, and
pulling-boat molds,
                 to be able to find,
for whatever it's worth,
                    what has to be there:
the requisite tool
              in this culch there's no end to:
the drawshave buried in potwarp,
chain, and manila jibsheets,
                   or, under the bench,
the piece that already may fit
                 the idea it begins
to shape up:
            not to be put off by split rudders,
stripped outboards, half
a gasket, and nailslick garboards:
                 to forget for good
all the old year's losses,
             save for
what needs be retrieved:
             a life given to
how today feels:
            to make of what's here
what has to be made
to make do.

Olga Broumas

Absence Of Noise   Presence Of Sound

for Kim Stafford

The river's blue where it reflects the sky
brown where mountain flat out long
miles I know I drove them
here

Lean on them silent in the dust listen dry
particles lift to my nostrils
lips

Impossible to tell the silence from the breathing
insects lungs sagebrush breathing in
of winds I here grateful
to be trying

This a desire
not only in the mind
but how the muscle swivels
onto bone how heart wills the auricle
floods and its altered rate

The doorway with the mirror
appears
I have been warned

No wall no door no post no mirror
Still the same highway scooped out with a knife
still the same river
Begin again
this time without choosing

I enter pretending it's a dream inscribed dust of dream
stroke stroke sign mountain name a name so excited I wake
myself who had been counting
on that

Oh the dream the moist the scaffolded prepared white wall
dream of a fresco

Charles Bukowski

A Love Poem For All The Women I Have Known

all the women
all their kisses the
different ways they love and
talk and need
things

their ears they all have
these ears and
vaginas and throats and dresses
and shoes and
bathrooms and automobiles and x-
husbands.

mostly
all the women are very
warm they remind me of
buttered toast with the butter
melted
in.

there is a similar look in the
eye: they have been
taken they have been
fooled. I don't know quite what to
do for them.

I am
a fair cook and a good
listener
but I never learned to
dance-- I was busy
then with larger things or,
at least, more
desperate.

but I've enjoyed their different
beds
smoking cigarettes
staring at the
ceilings. I was neither vicious nor
unfair. only
a student.

I know that they all have these
feet and barefoot they go across the floors as
I watch their bashful buttocks in the

dark. I know that they like me, some even
love me
but I love very
few.

some give me oranges and pills, fairly
stimulating; others talk quietly of
childhood and fathers and
landscapes; some are almost
crazy but none of them are without
force or meaning; some love
well, others not
so; the best at sex are not always the
best in other
ways; each has limits as I have
limits and we learn
each other
quickly.

all the women all the
women all the
bedrooms the
rolls of toilet
paper the rugs the
photos the
tapestries, it's
something like a church only
at times there's much
laughter.

these ears these
arms these
elbows these eyes
looking the fondness and
the waiting I have been
held I have been
held.

Hayden Carruth

Contra Mortem

> *"Thirty spokes unite in one nave,*
> *and because of the part where nothing is*
> *we have the use of a wheel."*
> *-Lao-tse*

The Being

Wherever shadow falls wherever the drowning
of darkness in great light takes waking under
and still awake and still alldiscerning
reaching as if to enter
in anysoever passages or subsurfaces burning
like a dry film upon the inner attaining
of earth of leaf of water of stone
of blood There murmuring in the din
of a talontaken grievance There in a flood
seething or in the rattle
of dry snowseas There trembling for the mood
of hysterical winds deceitful thistles
meteors blooming There in the huge fire
that rusts every thing away the opening middle
where the world falls in forever There There.

The Woman

Among birches moving in their white halfnakedness
she dances And the veils of her being obscure her
or half obscure her for they are her dress
or her undress while nearer
or farther she dances moving effortless
and selfabsorbed like the birches with their sense
of naturalness and when she appears
naked at last having cast to the breeze
her semblances as in her dreams the birches
step intricately before her
or drench her in cooling shadows all the riches
of this presence flowing upon her and through her
making her an object in the true world unknowable
her dance the dance of things without past or future
given and perfect and beyond and inconsolable.

The Child

Otherwise considered being is a force
more or less welldirected Cometh the child
exploded running nine ways at once
an egg dropped a cup spilled
a universe erupting hell on wheels whence

31

backward rocking he incautiously squints
in the village square of the square village
to the spire up up and up verge
upon verge higher and higher till he sits
in his damp britches plop
extended a being from his arse to his three wits
real to ideal and then gets up
weeping his laughter dancing his stumble worlding
every unworld eating names in his soup
lowest of low quickest unlife the immense lordling.

The Trees

Birches birches birches true and white
demure of habit and standing on ceremony
bending there left or right
a grove a classical harmony
and yet some secret moves among them Light
quivers Is it the aspens twinkling The night
come up reining a dark breeze
ruffling the spirit and the near trees
quicken sparkle vanish to the forest
among dogwood and elm
spruce and balsam viburnum and sweet locust
beech rockmaple tamarack alder
a congress a quiet congress for not one leaf intrudes
predominantly   Yet this repose this calm
this being fills the night of the living woods.

The Brook

A threefold obstacle   The center rock
so enormous only a glacial hand could lift it
or settle it in this bed   The hemlock
fallen long since and drifted
into the wide right cleft between rock and bank
stripped by the current denuded of limbs and bark
and yet still green emerald green
with moss and its great crest newgrown
among cardinal flowers   Then in the narrower channel
on the left an iron pot
out at the bottom and at last forever full
The stone the flower the artifact
to mark the brookfall singing flutes in the trees
music never faltering always exact
rising falling in the remote black seas.

The Mountain Fastness

Beyond and farther and yet from every vantage
rising eternally near crag above crag
this is the upthrust   A tossed village
lies like a trampled flag
at its feet and up there look the ridge
sloughs off the stunted firs like the very selvedge
of earth itself raveled and frayed
where the ground peels back   Call it the void
pulled inside out or the universal grain
in a mindless exultation
sprung from the notgrain   Its climbers learn
footholds too far apart and their own impatience
and death in the dark drops   Call it a comprising
call it the center and edge of every relation
the journeyer's pivot and the journeyer's horizon.

The Village

Twilight drivels down the mountain   There below
in slowly gathering shadow the lights come on
lighted windows vague and yellow
and very old   The town
is flecked with light except in the deep hollow
where the graves sink down   Hallowed white and narrow
the steeple rises under a copper fish
swimming in final roselight   The dutch
elm beetle carries his little burden from tree
to tree   Somewhere a dog
barks petulantly across a steel guitar
Ah it is all extraordinarily nostalgic
as people find who come from the city
to fret beneath the police magistrate's famous hatrack
that was the last caribou and now is a pity.

The Fall

Still after the clapper cracked the bell
after the suffocating complicity of the riot
summer's strangling tangling toil
still there came quiet
the colors of meditation in the fall
twilight and robins chirping still and all
potatoes and butternuts laid by
the old bees dreaming how to die
in a drunken reverie by the dripping press

and asters and goldenrod
murmuring darklights through the sleepiness
of completed things   After the blade
had driven through the eye and spilled the gold
something was won some recompense was had
in the histories of anguish quietly told.

The Great Death

Oh if a thousand old folk looked askance
when a puff of cyanide like a colorless wind
seized their gentle world
                              so and
                                  so
                                      who else
observed it   Yet behind
the customary daylight the small dance
of twinkling leaves had darkened and the scenes
that were revisited and tales retold
were not the same   Strangely the world
looked empty and strangely distant as if the stones
themselves had grown absentminded
and had forfeited their presence yet the suns
rose the moons set and people were openhanded
or closefisted as before   The children went back
to school where a few of them comprehended
that what was called their questing was their lack.

The Little Death

Falling plummeting unexpectedly sickeningly
through the region of grey cloud inhabited
by floating objects such as an eye
that grows on a stem a bed
hopping like a rabbit a glass finger a tray
of rings and minnows an artificial boy
a pistol   Descending through this
in rolling qualming swoops helpless
filled with nausea until far far down
far in a distant night
the clouds open on a dark pool and then
a reflected star   With a desolate
cry falling falling falling into the star
the candleflame the spark and through and out
in the noplace where all the nothings never are.

The Coming of Snow

Along the denuded aisles a shadow walks
casting no body bending no branch nor cracking
one dry twig   It sighs and talks
or maybe only the bracken
is mumbling in the wind nothing or no one takes
the time to care   The snow comes a few flakes
unobserved then thicker softening
the raw air almost as in the spring
apple petals falling diffuse the sun
but cold and with a tang
of reality   And though at first they seem to run
him through and vanish on his tongue
slowly he takes an outline and footprints show
the passage he has truly made among
the rubble graces brightening in the snow.

The Moon

Reflected light reflected again on snow
but beauty is lonely lonely   The snowsurface
is hard gleaming vitrescent blue
without crest or crevice
extending beyond anywhere for long ago
the horizon crumbled in an indeterminate glow
and the night has stillness   Light
that is fragile paleolithic white
from this fossilshell embedded in a sky of shale
conveys a snowgleaming
track for the solitary on and on a trial
of his sole desperation climbing
the world of pure beauty   Remote and high
a real light glimmers an upland farmstead shining
or only a star in the unhorizoned sky.

The Book

Pure beauty is pure being and pure being
is freedom in its most desperate purity
Winter was taintless pythagorean
and meaningless   Then why
was freedom in its purity so unfreeing
why was the world and its lovely snow a thing
so merely coercive like a page

white and unrealized why must rage
in responsibility choose the which and when
and where for each impress
of something particular some character   The pen
wrote freedom's elegy nothing less
than ultimate aggrievement for the cost
of mind's disablement in loneliness
and for the natural things so wrongly lost.

The Thaw

Rigidity nonlife the meaning neither of life
nor of unlife neither a presence nor an absence
but the snowworld the compacted snow and ice
so powerful that the granite
formed in the nuclear sun clicks like the dice
in a crapshooter's hand and shatters a white
incumbency white being the color
of hardness as in the unusual power
of iridium a lithic ideal gripping the forest
in petrifaction bringing
the encompassing the silence the sidereal frost
not just an antisound but a singing
of nothing a reciting of nevertobeborn until
whether near or remote auspicious or menacing
the water by drop by drop by drop begins to fall.

The Stone

Difficult to think of a stone's gratitude
difficult for that matter to think of stone
essences so various   The white shade
cast by the winter moon
withdraws into covert places and the multiflood
of earthlight often darkly or in tones subdued
by interspersion slowly drenches
the forest the brook the stone   Birches
step forward and the stone rises like an earthspirit
snow dripping from its flanks
burnished and new but scarcely changed a merit
of the abiding between the banks
marking the upstream from down   Its warmth is taken
from another source yet such warmtaking links
the primal act with this   So the woods waken.

The Water

The brook had been frozen almost everywhere   Mounds
of snow had covered the ice serene
and cool as corpseflesh while quiet small sounds
came from the holes where the skein
of black water continued winding   But now
only the scraps and tatters of the snow
are left on the banks and the water
seems purged of darkness brighter
than its winding immanence   In the shallows
where pebbles excite the current
the brook is shaken like the quivering lightandshadow
of aspenleaves or like the cadence
of hundreds of migrant wings flashing in sunlight
against the flow forever far from their nests
and singing singing so pleasantly in their flight.

The Leaves

If the sky were green instead of blue its green
would be the aspenleaves which have the same
inlighted sweet intensity of tone
and are the first to come
in spring closefollowed by hickory ash hawthorn
and the rest with butternut last   Each has its own
conception of green some yellow some blue
some like the rockmaple reddish nor
is any leaf precisely like any other
Their tide assaults the mountain
by way of the gradual foothills   Greening breakers
lunge and snap at the heights counting
the evenings forest by forest until the waves
splash on the far high summit announcing
the actual world in the heyday of the leaves.

The Primavera

Through the forest across the fair hills away
to compagnas glistening to deltas sparkling
in the suns of finer canticles to the bois
to the luckenwalde to arden
to the name of every woods sung in a heartcry
see the dog run   Light as a wish free
as a thought he runs with his nose to the ground
raising his bellvoice gone and returned

on his keen inquisitive course as swift as an echo
and the prints of his paws are flowers
and the shaking of his coat is the soft rain and the glow
of his eyes is the making of nests his terror
is the scourging of somnolence for he is the dog of spring
and in his going and his returning lie the powers
of extension and concretion that make and remake all being.

The Woman's Genitals

Oh this world and oh this dear worldbody
see how it has become become become
how it has flowered and how it has put on gaudy
appearances how it is a plum
in its ripening a rose in its reddening a berry
in its glittering a finch in its throbbing a cowry
in its extraordinary allusiveness a night
of midsummer in its fragrance a tide
in its deepsurging and a dark woodland spring
in its concealing sources
see how it is velvety how its innerness clings
and presses how nearly it repulses
how it then takes and cherishes how it is austere
how it is free how it reviles abuses
and how it is here and how it was always here.

The Sun

Such a reasonable irrational fellow goodhumored
and reliable too since the occasional scorching
is someone else's fault   No wonder
the ancients frankly adored him
and if their solemnity seems now simpleminded
nevertheless he is highly esteemed and honored
more than sometimes appears   A landlord
who never asks for the rent is hardly
to be despised   And what does he care for
but to be good company
with everything and to promote the common welfare
by maintaining the regularity
of public occasions   Unhappily although he desires
nothing but calm and abhors the solitary
he dwells alone burning with a million fires.

The Child's Being

Extended and always uncentered which is why it scares
everyone but him   When an insistent finger
stabs him with a you he only stares
uncomprehendingly a stranger
to the pronominal itch and then pointing anywhere
to the tree the cloud the flower distant or near
expostulates in manic delight
me me me a spendthrift spate
of consciousness   And thus the child puts on
his being as the dark world
in its necessity puts on the dawn
by turning toward it   The child
trembling in halflight giving himself away
becomes sun's favor the choice of what is not willed
a being freeborn and intricate like the day.

The Being as Memory

A carpet raveling on the loom a girl
with a widowspeak and misty legs a moon
like a fisheye rising from a pool
a black longwinging loon
bursting afire in the sunset a torn sail
groveling in a wave a whisper in a stairwell
a helmet upturned in the black rain
and later a star reflected a coin
glimmering on seastones a sound of motors
and machineguns
in the dawn a kiss and candleflame a sonata
for clarinet a bone cracking a woman
wearing a blue veil and in kashan in a room
where the little darkeyed weaving girls lay down
and died a carpet raveling on a loom.

The Being as Moment

Between a sea and a sea where the combers meet
in the cancellations of their endless breaking
between a dream and a dream where the night
arrests in eternal waking
between two notes of a thracian song where the flute
stops and an infinite stillness opens what
is it where is it what and where
oh sea and dream and song   Will the blurred

images surging ever fill the abyss
toward which they flow   Sighing
in the long languid tango of their kiss
will the lovers on that continually dying
wave of sensation ever really know
what they know their drift and their expiring
between a sea and a sea in the faint starglow?

The Being as Prevision

The mindseye is flitting like a moth among summer firs
the palewhite slowfast moth that threads the burning
pillars of the hidden sun and fares
tricklingly over the ferny
firesplashes of the forest bed among whorls
of misty gold rising in aureoles
under the branches   There the veeries
whistle the variations of a curious
doubling echoing note and the ovenbirds
shriek surprising hallelujahs
in unseen transepts   There the filigree ferns
the moccasin flowers the great trees
and the palewhite moth are a lucency in the semidusk
of causeless light until through a gap the source
burns burns for a dazzling instant and then turns blank.

The Ecstasy

Dawn will be the time and the forest will be the place
the brook the stone in their arrest and flowing
turning perpetually in the kind of grace
that is simply a kind of knowing
intensified around this present   The woman's face
halfsmiling against the stone will seal the force
of the lordly surging flooding sun
entering with her husbandman
entering surging flooding and yet not seen
and never to be told.   The brook
its music almost lost or too serene
for her to hear will in its small crook
fold her on the stone   Her strange halfsmile
as if the earth had found its generic look
will stay upon the stone a long long while.

The Summer

Cicadas blur the ear as the blue heat haze
blurs the eye   Fulfillment is a word
known to be lucky and hence not nice
or perhaps a shade absurd
Wise folk avoid it though they may speak of days
of changing tension   Softly the hayfields rise
in the seedtime's changing browns and rusts
to the green mountain where the farthest crests
blur in purple boundaries like the child's
outreaching perceptions
and fall back in media gloria like the folds
of the woman's experience   The redwings
the meadowlarks the treeswallows zoom in the warmth
small and sudden pleasant interconnections
uniting all this knowledge with the earth.

The Nothing I

Look in the flower deep in the tulip cup
where the redness sinks in a still whirlwind of black
look in the stone look in the drop
of water or look back
or forward to the moon or the sun or look up
to the wells of the sky look down the hot strip
of the highway straightening forever
or in the glass gone blank and silver
of the cars plunging past look in the socket
of the candlestick or in that
of the shotglass look in the empty gauntlet or look
in the clamshell or in the straw hat
of the president look well in the book
whose perfect lines string out so black and flat
look at the cigarette smoke rising look look

The Nothing II

where the child's eyes glaze with memory where the man's glaze
with forknowledge and how they darken and alter
to vacancy as when the shifting breeze
ramps like a closing shutter
on the deeplighted bay look in the woman's eyes
bravely in her moment of rapture when the skies
loom between her lashes or look there
in the mirror at those eyes bend closer

and closer still look in the black pupils
where other eyes appear
and in them others infinitely infinitely pools
of incomprehension look the fear
is nothing look the courage nothing the song
has no consequence look look it is here
nothing nothing nothing nothing nothing.

The Wheel of Being I

Changing figures   The dionysian child
the woman in her assurances the old town   ·
in its hallucinations spilled
like dominoes the mountain
and the void the moon and the sun whirled
from misthidden vale to vale and the day coiled
in the forest   A word is like an ant
·dragging a dead spider the meant
and the unmeant   So upon ragged changing seas
the poem which is a ship
buoyed by its hollowness on the abstruse
coordinates of meaning carries the loop
of its horizon forever with it   Scan
this circle vanishing across the deep
It is contrived it is actual it is a man.

The Wheel of Being II

Such figures if they succeed are beautiful
because for a moment we brighten in a blaze of rhymes
and yet they always fail and must fail
and give way to other poems
in the endless approximations of what we feel
Hopeless it is hopeless   Only the wheel
endures   It spins and spins winding
the was the is the willbe out of nothing
and thus we are   Thus on the wheel we touch
each to each a part
of the great determining reality   How much
we give to one another   Perhaps our art
succeeds after all our small song done in the faith
of lovers who endlessly change heart for heart
as the gift of being   Come let us sing against death.

Raymond Carver

Luck

I was nine years old.
I had been around liquor
all my life. My friends
drank too, but they
could handle it.
We'd take cigarettes, beer,
a couple of girls
and go out to the fort.
We'd act silly.
Sometimes you'd pretend
to pass out so the girls
could examine you.
They'd put their hands
down your pants while
you lay there trying
not to laugh, or else
they would lean back,
close their eyes, and
let you feel them all over.
Once at a party my dad
came to the back porch
to take a leak.
We could hear voices
over the record player,
see people standing around
laughing and drinking.
When my dad finished,
he zipped up, stared a while
at the starry sky —
it was always starry then
on summer nights —
and went back inside.
The girls had to go home.
I slept all night in the fort
with my best friend.
We kissed on the lips
and touched each other.
I saw the stars fade
toward morning,
I saw a woman sleeping on our lawn.
I looked up her dress,
then I had a beer
and a cigarette.
Friends, I thought this
was living.
Indoors, someone
had put out a cigarette

in a jar of mustard.
I had a straight shot
from the bottle, then
a drink of warm collins mix,
then another whiskey.
And though I went from room
to room, nobody was home.
What luck I thought.
Years later,
I still wanted to give up
friends, love, starry skies,
for a house where nobody
was home, and all I could drink.

Philip Dacey

Form Rejection Letter

We are sorry we cannot use the enclosed.
We are returning it to you.
We do not mean to imply anything by this.
We would prefer not to be pinned down about this matter.
But we are not keeping — cannot, will not keep —
    what you sent us.
We did receive it, though, and our returning it to you
    is a sign of that.
It was not that we minded your sending it to us
    unasked.
That is happening all the time, they
    come when we least expect them,
      when we forget we have needed or might yet need them,
    and we send them back.
We send this back.
It is not that we minded.
At another time, there is no telling...
But this time, it does not suit our present needs.

We wish to make it clear it was not easy receiving it.
It came so encumbered.
And we are busy here.
We did not feel
    we could take it on.
We know it would not have ended there.
It would have led to this, and that.
We know about these things.
It is why we are here.
We wait for it. We recognize it when it comes.
Regretfully, this form letter does not allow us to elaborate
    why we send it back.
It is not that we minded.

We hope this does not discourage you. But we would not
    want to encourage you falsely.
It requires delicate handling, at this end.
If we had offered it to you,
    perhaps you would understand.
But, of course, we did not.
You cannot know what your offering it
    meant to us,
And we cannot tell you:
There is a form we must adhere to.
It is better for everyone that we use this form.

As to what you do in future,
   we hope we have given you signs,
   that you have read them,
   that you have not mis-read them.
We wish we could be more helpful.
But we are busy.
We are busy returning so much.
We cannot keep it.
It all comes so encumbered.
And there is no one here to help.
Our enterprise is a small one.
We are thinking of expanding.
We hope you will send something.

Madeline DeFrees

First-Class Relics: Letter to Dennis Finnell *

I wanted to wear your name religiously for the rest
of my life, asked over and over,
spending my threepenny choices on Lucky Bites
from the general store. We understood fooling around
could be serious, the way our crippled uncles
coined arias. One day I heard bells
celebrate angels called to their given names. My plot
to ring one for you went flat, patron
beheaded by the fat music director's stubby hands.
She said we might bring luster
to that holy handle, but she wouldn't like it,
identity sunk--mud or menace--in slang.

                                    It was slang
breaking out in a rush of letters I couldn't write
from the old enclosure, my mail censored. Dreams
turned out, patched comforters to air. I thought of you,
though, coughing and blinking, dipping your Sunday face
with the others. And I heard the tall
unhappy note of your voice
catwalk the trestle, drawn by the owl in your mama's
boot. We were deep in 'mad water,' all right,
flaunting that scrappy Irish kin
I tried to adopt as a child. I loved the straight
line of your mouth, uncertain French
asides sneaking out from balloon characters.

Good thing you didn't flinch when balloons rode
circus track to the old Hotel, and you went along.
Deranged pots lined your mama's stoop
and kettles, black on pink linoleum. Over the cracked
lintel, azaleas burned, twin red spots
in the pale of your face. I keep a diary of what we
learned. You were thrifty with letters, using them
more than once, a new address every week. "Is it
one or two?" I'd say, plopping them in like sugar lumps.
Two. First, last and always. Oh, you
were a deep one. I've rhymed your name with an Iowa
town ever since.

                        Once shaking off the town dust, you
headed for the Roman wine god, our letters
always crossing, mostly missing. That didn't work,
neither did you. You tried the Parisian bishop's act,
head carried in his own two hands.
Pastoral letters. You were good enough to shake
the basilica over the tomb of your betters, the green

* Author of the "Fool" poems and "Letters from the Hotel de Dream"

night we met under the clown's umbrella. I knew
I had to change. We planned my tough escape by moonlight.
The day your daddy bit the bullet, I put
your name on the map. You'll find seven worn-out letters
by the date book next to the calendar of martyrs.

Stephen Dobyns

The Delicate, Plummeting Bodies

A great cry went up from the stockyards and
slaughterhouses, and Death, tired of complaint
and constant abuse, withdrew to his underground garage.
He was still young and his work was a torment.
All over, their power cut, people stalled like street cars.
Their gravity taken away, they began to float.
Without buoyancy, they began to sink. Each person
became a single darkened room. The small hand
pressed firmly against the small of their backs
was suddenly gone and people swirled to a halt
like petals fallen from a flower. Why hurry?
Why get out of bed? People got off subways,
on subways, off subways all at the same stop.
Everywhere clocks languished in antique shops
as their hands composed themselves in sleep.
Without time and decay, people grew less beautiful.
They stopped sleeping and spent weeks following stray dogs.
The first to react were remnants of the church.
They falsified miracles: displayed priests posing
as corpses until finally they sneezed or grew lonely.
Then governments called special elections to choose those
to join the ranks of the volunteer dead: unhappy people
forced to sit in straight chairs for weeks at a time.
Interest soon dwindled. Then the army seized power
and soldiers ran through the street dabbing the living
with red paint. You're dead, they said. Maybe
tomorrow, people answered, today we're just breathing:
look at the sky, look at the color of the grass.
For without Death each color had grown brighter.
At last a committee of businessmen met together,
because with Death gone money had no value.
They went to where Death was waiting in a white room,
and he sat on the floor and looked like a small boy
with pale blond hair and eyes the color of clear water.
In his lap was a red ball heavy with the absence of life.
The businessmen flattered him. We will make you king,
they said. I am king already, Death answered. We will
print your likeness on all the money of the world.
It is there already, Death answered. We adore you
and will not live without you, the businessmen said.
Death said, I will consider your offer.

How Death was restored to his people:

At first the smallest creatures began to die —
bacteria and certain insects. No one noticed. Then fish
began to float to the surface; lizards and tree toads
toppled from sun-warmed rocks. Still no one saw them.
Then birds began tumbling out of the air,
and as sunlight flickered on the blue feathers
of the jay, brown of the hawk, white of the dove,
then people lifted their heads and pointed to the sky
and from the thirsty streets cries of welcome rose up
like a net to catch the delicate and plummeting bodies.

Norman Dubie

The Pennacesse Leper Colony
For Women. Cape Cod. 1922.

The island, you mustn't say, had only rocks and scrub pine;
Was on a blue, bright day like a blemish in this landscape.
And Charolette who is frail and the youngest of us collects
Sticks and branches to start our fires, cries as they burn
Because they resemble most what she has lost
Or has little of: long fingers, her toes
And a left arm gone past the elbow, soon clear to her shoulder.
She has the mouth of sea perch. Five of our sisters wear
Green hoods. You are touched by all of this, *but not by us.*
To be touched by us; to be kissed! Sometimes
We see couples rowing in the distance in yellow coats.

Sometimes they fish with handlines; we offend
Everyone who are offended most
And by everything and everyone. The five goats love us, though,
And live in our dark houses. When they are
Full with milk they climb the steps and beg that
They be milked. Their teats brush the steps and leave thick
Yellow trails of fresh milk. We are all females here.
Even the ghosts. We must wash, of course, in saltwater
But it smarts or maybe it even hurts us. Often with a rope
Around her waist Anne is lowered entirely into the water.
She splashes around and screams in pain. Her screams
Sometimes carry clear to the beaches on the Cape.

For us I say so often. For us we say. *For us!* We are
Human and not individual, we hold everything in common.
We are individual, you could pick us out in a crowd.
You did. This island is not our prison. We are not kept
In; not even by our skin.

Once Anne said she would love to be a negro or a trout.

We live without you. *Father,* I don't know why I have written
You all this; but be proud for I am living, and yet each day
I am less and less your flesh. Someday, eventually, you
Should only think of me as being a lightning bug on the lawn,
Or the negro fishing at the pond, or the fat trout he wraps
In leaves that he is showing to someone. I'll be

Most everything for you. And I'll be gone.

Richard Eberhart

To Alpha Dryden Eberhart
November 26, 1977, on being seventy-five.

When you were in high school, in the old red brick
Building, a bomb in the form of a firecracker
Went off under your seat in the schoolroom. The
Teacher thought you were the culprit, you were
Summoned and you were expelled, although your sense
Of fairness to a friend kept you from telling
That another had set off the report. Then up rose
Our fair and gentle mother, roused to go before
The school committee to attest that her son was
Not a bad boy. Bravo for her. It took courage,
But she stood by you as a youth of good character,
No revolutionary. Over half a century later
I recall this prank, its gusto, and the high sense
Of life that inhered in you and in our mother.

Another memory, when we used to go down in the meadow
Somewhere near the river, and snare gophers. We had no
Sense of their pain or of our injustice. We were boys
Out for sport. A circle of string was placed over the hole,
Run back maybe thirty feet and there on our bellies
We youths would wait for a long time for an unwary head
To pop into sight. Zing, and we would strangle the creature,
Stand up and swing him around our heads in gusty triumph.
Then we would skin him and nail him to a board and
Salt him, and in a while have a number of such trophies.

Pigeons

If a scientist had bred pigeons the size of horses, they
had great masterly breasts with pink pigeon nipples; and they
strutted, and cooed with voices as deep as bulls...

They were soft, like stuffed furniture designed for huge
cripples.

And the scientist had to cut them open to make sure there
wasn't money hidden in their stuffings.

They would be like the terrible mother when they tilted
their heads, staring one-eyed; their great masterly breasts,
so soft; their pink pigeon nipples...

And the scientist would really have to think about cutting
them open to see if Benjamin Franklin wasn't flying his kite
in the thunderstorms of their breasts...

Alan Feldman

The Personals

My wife reads them. She wants to keep abreast of what's available
Like a person who owns a house but still follows real estate.
I imagine her back on the market, because I've died
Or I've slept through garbage day again
Or one fatal time too often I've turned away in our bed
Insisting on the right of a depressed, anxious person
To freedom from happiness --
The happiness she is always trying to give me.
And how would she advertise? Humorous, carefree man needed
For a life without inexplicable descents?

When she comes back exhilarated from evening class
And tells me all the dirty jokes she's heard in carpool
Like the one about "How do you know if elephants have been copulating
        in your back yard at night?"
And she turns to me in the dark and tells me she has the hots for me
And I just want to be alone in my bitterness
And she just wants to romp with someone in her liveliness
I think of the personals

                And I surrender
Though I'll be damned if I'll talk to her
And I concentrate on stretching apart my toes
And letting the pleasure sparks dart around between them.

She doesn't seem to notice how furiously quiet I am
And anyway, I'm not furious
I'm a sour, sensitive thirty-five year old writer/teacher
Searching for an attractive, even-tempered woman interested in the arts

And as well-mated as I'll ever be
I drop off to sleep. In the morning she rises to our son's first cries
And I rise to the groans of the garbage truck
And think about nothing I was so blackly thinking of last night
Except how you can know elephants have been copulating in the back yard

Because you get up in the morning and find that some of the trashcan liners
        are missing.

Carolyn Forché

Reunion

> *Just as he changes himself, in the end*
> *eternity changes him.*
>   -Mallarme

On the phonograph, the voice
of a woman already dead for three
decades, singing of a man
who could make her do anything.
On the table, two fragile
glasses of black wine,
a bottle wrapped in its towel.
It is that room, the one
we took in every city, it is
as I remember: the bed, a block
of moonlight and pillows.
My fingernails, pecks of light
on your thighs.
The stink of the fire escape.
The wet butts of cigarettes
you crushed one after another.
How I watched the morning come
as you slept, more my son
than a man ten years older.
How my breasts feel, years
later, the tongues swishing
in my dress, some yours, some
left by other men.
Since then, I have always
wakened first, I have learned
to leave a bed without being
seen and have stood
at the wash basins, wiping
oil and salt from my skin,
staring at the cupped water
in my two hands.
I have kept everything
you whispered to me then.
I can remember it now as I see you
again, how much tenderness we could
wedge between a stairwell
and a police lock, or as it was,
as it still is, in the voice
of a woman singing of a man
who could make her do anything.

Bird-Window-Flying

If we had been given names to love
each other by, I would take this one
from you, bird flying all day
in my woodhouse. The door
is open as when you came
to it, into it, as
space between branches. "Never
trust doors," you tell the window,
the small of your body flung
against the white bay.

At dusk, when I walked in
with my armload of green alder,
I could see the memory of light
shining water through your wings. You
were gray with it. The window
had aged you with promises.
I thought the boats, the gulls
should have stilled you
by now. When I cupped

my hands in their shadows, warm
over the heartwings, I saw the skin
of light between my fingers
haloed and glowing. Three steps I
took with you, for
you— three light-years travelling
to your sky, beak
and claw of you, the soft burr of flight
at my fingerbones.

If I take a lover for every tree, I
will not have again such an opening as
when you flew from me.

I have gone in to build my fire. All
the walls, all the
wings of my house are burning. The flames
of me, the long hair
unbraiding.

Brendan Galvin

The Old Trip By Dream Train

Engine and tender, old loaf-shaped Pullman.
I am making the trip alone
because of the house a dream within this dream
keeps erecting in my sleep.

It is always barely April, but at loading docks
behind the church-topped mills, in the cinders
and shattered weeds, it is late November.

No one is on the streets, no one's not working,
and the workday flashing past looks empty,
the storefronts blind. Not one pane of forty-eight
in a factory window winks; just row on row,
banked like the pigeonholes
in a postal clerk's nightmare.

In a side yard a hairless, vested man
rakes among shadows eloquent as the clang
of steel doors. There are joined angles of bridges,
tanks with coolie hats, a distant refinery
like stacked poker chips,

but always that house, white in April sunlight,
nearly perfect except for broken slats
in the green, nailed shutters.

Then the piney backs of towns, and blond fields
where rocks seem to crawl out of their shadows,
and the slow progressions into small identical
cities of brown bungalows and triple-deckers,
clatter of Redcap's dollies, arrival and departure

through which I see the shadow of a crow
crossing white shingles in light so clear
it could be bottled and sold.

Switchyards and sidings, men working gears
with levers, municipal power blocks, trestles,
at one stop the illusion of slipping back
when the cars alongside begin to move;

finally the coast, where a tug trundles upriver
and one seabird crosses high and slow,
a hint of prehistory in its flight,

then cranberry bogs, ditch-ruled and crossed
with levees supporting pump houses,
a set of iron wheels stunned in sunlight.

I try to see the roof of that white place,
the red brick chimney's shadow,
the rainstreak of mortar like a second shadow.

Under cirrus brushwork the creeks
crawl into harbors, their soft tides
feeling seaward in various blues, opening out
under sky opening out.

Crossings too small for gates and lanterns blur by,
each with its warning X,
and one by one, joined by railside wires,
minor stations appear on the line,

a country of white houses whose one story
bedrooms and late ells meet their barns,
whose oil drums sit on sawhorses.

I stop this trip by its pullcord, and step down
to a sooty cream station trimmed in maroon,
a coalbox alongside, and walk up a two-lane road
nothing is moving on.

The light is always April, chilled amber,
the air headier than I imagined.
Beyond the Big Dipper Dancehall, torn
to its baseposts thirty years ago,

I turn onto a sand road, pass cabins shut
till June, and Ed Mather's place;
he elected to live up hollow from everything
but a deer run and weather.

If I find that house where locust trees
shadow the flaking paint,
will I pry its green storm door and break
the frosted pane over the inside knob,

and enter rooms abandoned to mothballs and
mousedirt and that gray matter that springs out
on old shoes, and call that warehouse
of sheeted furniture home?

Gary Gildner

Today They Are Roasting Rocky Norse

Today they are roasting Rocky Norse.
Me, today they are roasting me
while I sit here, dead from the belt down.
But hey! Look at these trousers. Black Nickle
born with a ball in his palms, Mr. Real Fine Hands,
he'd say Man those are fly pants, man. Fly.
& wiggle both flat hands down by his hams
cooling everything. Black Nickle. Who came in grim & gray
when they propped me up in all those good pillows, all that
pretty gash flashing their choppers around my head, pop, pop
ROCKY NORSE IS FIGHTING BACK. Gray, man, he was *ash*.

I like pork, always have. Small it boys
& tell me what is better, clean sweat pants
or a woman from South Dakota — from someplace
you never heard of — keeping it warm in the parking lot.
Her old man raised sheep but she raised the moon
raised it up & gave it over. Fly, Mr. Rocky.
Or clean socks & no god damn throbbing
knees & shoulders when it rains.
I'll tell you what I liked about that woman.
She could drive all day over South Dakota
& two more hours over Minnesota
& still raise the moon soft & mellow.

I remember one time I looked in the sky over Red Oak
& he threw me a horse-wink, the grinning fool.
Another time grabbing that salamander,
it was so orange she wanted to eat it.
Pump pump went its throat. Pump pump pump.
Finally I put it down. Go on, get out of here.
Go raise some big kids that can tackle.
South Dakota said Rocky you are my man.
South Dakota said that, her & her funny dreams.

Somewhere water's dripping on a sink full of nylons.
Another beer? Sure, give it here. & when my baggie's full
kid you can empty it, how's that? Today is my day.
Roasting Rocky. & the smoke going up from that hog
is going up all over the Midwest, going up over St. Cloud
Bemidji & even Dee-troit where Snake hauled his buns
out of & tore over my ass one time so quick & beautiful
nothing would ever stop him & nothing did, the greaser
safety wet his pants just straining to watch I believe.

What was that dream she had down in Dallas? God yes
she said Rocky you carried around a sack of darkness

like a sack of black dirt & you tied it next to your belly.
I said how about a sack of money honey, but she went on
those green eyes big & wide & all that red hair falling
everywhere, saying I laid down with it & stroked the folds
like I wanted it to take me in.

Wake up baby, I am here! ROCKY NORSE the sign says
& the arrow is pointing straight at that hog
I am getting the first piece of. Free.
Along with all the Hamms I can pour in my baggie.
& everyone's shown up except those two bastards
who were raised on ears & lips & parts
no one can stand to even look at.
But I guess I spook Nickle
& maybe Snake is dead. Which I can say I am glad
I am not. Hey listen. All that sponge they cut from my knees,
what difference does it make to me now?

You get used to everything. If I could do it
without spitting up all over my tie
I'd lead a cheer. OK fans
gimme ah *you*!
gimme ah *get*!
gimme ah *get-used-to-EVERYTHING*!

South Dakota swing your smooth moon up here
next to my King Daddy Seat of Honor
& tell the folks about that seed you
found on the sheet between your dimpled knees.
What'd it look like baby?
A kidney bean Rocky & it was breathing
I wanted to put it back in
but I couldn't & I couldn't
find anyone who would
I touched it Rocky
& it stopped breathing
a piece of paper, that's all it was
a piece of paper folded in half
no, I opened it up
Rocky it was a plastic sack
you were inside
all of your little pieces . . .

My first bike was a fat-tired job the Red Oak
Sears had to special order. & I know exactly
where that bike is today, it's frozen under
Crab Smoltz's hog barn. When they were all

standing around with their little pliers fixing my spine
I saw that fat-tired honey rising up shiny & new
from the wet cement I pushed it into, rising up
with the first good man who ever taped my ankles
glued to the seat & twisting those grips for
all he was worth, saying Rocky I got this machine
but it's too much! Take it off my hands!
So I took that shiny Red Flyer off Coker's
small swift hands & rose up past Crab Smoltz's
sun-roasted face & his hogs that looked just like him
& up past my old man saying quit running
those cows when they're full god dammit
up past Snake & South Dakota up past Nickle up past
the Mayflower truck that wouldn't move & the long
white line I laid my nose against thinking this is one
godawful wrong place to fall off
my brand new Harley & cream . . .

I think when God sits back & looks
at everything he made he gets
a hole in his gut.
I broke everything — neck & legs & both cheeks.
& buried half a chopper in my tongue.
Hey God you ever feel like a jerk?
You ever feel looking down at this handsome boy
who could open up holes for semis
who's got to tickle out his own crap now —
you ever feel like calling in sick?

Religion, my old man said he had all of it
he needed in two hundred head & no TB.
My mother went when somebody croaked. & baked something.
Snake said don't knock it man.
Right baby I don't knock it, I eat pork
I eat the hog you are not here to see my name on
along with all the boys & their trim women
who cut it up in little pieces
at twenty-five bucks a plate,
along with South Dakota & her red hair
falling all over those white shoulders.
I am eating pork with a hole in my tongue
hey Snake I am going down, my juice baby
my meat are making muscle. Tearing open
those slots baby, moving everything to one side
& coming back where they don't see us
they don't see us Snake but they smell something
real good going up over Red Wing going up

over Shenandoah over Winona over Dallas & New York City
they want in baby they are screaming their guts out
they want in so bad . . .

They want in where the water won't
quit dripping baby tell them how it is.
Tell them you are my turtle
you save my legs from the sharks.
But please don't say my heart is a peach
my heart is a bag of nuts somebody cut off
one of Crab's pigs, milky blue blood
is pumping it baby milky blue blood
tell them

Louise Glück

Lamentations

1. *The Logos*

They were both still,
the woman mournful, the man
branching into her body.

But god was watching.
They felt his gold eye
projecting flowers on the landscape.

Who knew what he wanted?
He was god, and a monster.
So they waited. And the world
filled with his radiance,
as though he wanted to be understood.

Far away, in the void that he had shaped,
he turned to his angels.

2. *Nocturne*

A forest rose from the earth.
O pitiful, so needing
God's furious love --

Together they were beasts.
They lay in the fixed
dusk of his negligence;
from the hills wolves came, mechanically
drawn to their human warmth,
their panic.

Then the angels saw
how He divided them:
the man, the woman, and the woman's body.

Above the churned reeds, the leaves let go
a slow moan of silver.

3. *The Covenant*

Out of fear, they built a dwelling place.
But a child grew between them
as they slept, as they tried
to feed themselves.

They set it on a pile of leaves,
the small discarded body
wrapped in the clean skin
of an animal. Against the black sky
they saw the massive argument of light.

Sometimes it woke. As it reached its hands
they understood they were the mother and father,
there was no authority above them.

4. *The Clearing*

Gradually, over many years,
the fur disappeared from their bodies
until they stood in the bright light
strange to one another.
Nothing was as before.
Their hands trembled, seeking
the familiar.

Nor could they keep their eyes
from the white flesh
on which wounds would show clearly
like words on a page.

And from the meaningless browns and greens
at last God arose, His great shadow
darkening the sleeping bodies of His children,
and leapt into heaven.

How beautiful it must have been,
the earth, that first time
seen from the air.

Linda Gregg

The Defeated

I sat at the desk for a while fooling with my hair
and looking at the black birds on the bakery roof.
Pulled the curtain, put my hair back, and said
it's time to start. Now it's after three.
You are still on the bus, I guess, looking out
the window. Sleeping. Knowing your defeat
and eating lunch part by part so it will last
the whole journey.

I heard there are women who light candles
and put them in the sand. Wade out in dresses
carrying flowers. Here we have no hope.
The pregnant woman has the abortion and then
refuses to speak. Horses stall in their strength,
whitening patches of air with their breath.
There will be this going on without them.
Dogs bark or five birds fly straight up
to a branch out of reach.

I had warm pumpernickle bread, cheese and chicken.
It is sunny outside. I miss you. My head is tired.
John was nice this morning. Already what I remember
most is the happiness of seeing you. Having tea.
Falling asleep. Waking up with you there awake
in the kitchen. It was like being alive twice.
I'll try to tell you better when I am stronger.

What does the moth think when the skin begins to split?
Is the air an astonishing pain? I keep seeing the arms
bent. The legs smashed up against the breasts,
with her sex showing. The weak hands clenched.
I see the sad, unused face. Then she starts to stand up
in the opening out. I know ground and trees.
I know air. But then everything else stops
because I don't know what happens after that.

Marilyn Hacker

La Fontaine De Vaucluse

for Marie Ponsot

Why write unless you praise the sacred places...
-Richard Howard: *"Audiences"*

1

Azure striation swirls beyond the stones
flung in by French papas and German boys.
The radio-guide emits trilingual noise.
"Always 'two ladies alone'; we were not alone."
Source, cunt, umbilicus, resilient blue
springs where the sheer gorge spreads wooded, mossed thighs;
unsounded female depth in a child-sized
pool boys throw rocks at. Hobbled in platform shoes,
girls stare from the edge. We came for the day
on a hot bus from Avignon. A Swed-
ish child hurls a chalk boulder; a tall girl,
his sister, twelve, tanned, crouches to finger shell-
whorls bedded in rock-moss. We find our way
here when we can; we take away what we need.

2

Here, when we can, we take what we need:
stones, jars of herb-leaves, scrap-patch workbags stored
in the haphazard rooms we can afford.
Marie and I are lucky: we can feed
our children and ourselves on what we earn.
One left the man who beat her, left hostages
two daughters; one weighs her life to her wages,
finds both wanting and, bought out, stays put, scorn-
ful of herself for not deserving more.
The concierge at *Le Regent* is forty-six;
there fifteen years, widowed for one, behind
counters a dun perpetual presence, fixed
in sallow non-age till Marie talked to her.
I learn she is coeval with my friends.

3

I learn she is coeval with my friends:
the novelist of seventy who gives
us tea and cakes; the sister with whom she lives
a dialogue; the old Hungarian
countess' potter daughter, British, dyke,
bravely espoused in a medieval hill
town in Provence; Jane whom I probably will
never know and would probably never like;
Liliane the weaver; Liliane's daughter
the weaver; Liliane's housewifely other

daughter, mothering; the great-grandmother
who drove us through gnarled lanes at Avignon;
the virgin at the source with wedgies on;
Iva, who will want to know what I brought her.

4

Iva, who will want to know what I brought her,
(from Selfridge's, a double-decker bus,
a taxi, Lego; a dark blue flowered dress
from Uniprix; a wickerwork doll's chair
from the Venice market; books; a wrapped-yarn deer;
a batik: girl guitarist who composes
sea-creatures, one of three I chose,
two by the pupil, one by the woman who taught her)
might plunge her arms to the elbows, might shy stones,
might stay shy. I'll see her in ten days.
Sometimes she still swims at my center; sometimes
she is a four-year-old an ocean away
and I am on vertiginous terrain
where I am nobody's mother and nobody's daughter.

5

"Where I am, nobody's mother and nobody's daughter
can find me," words of a woman in pain
or self-blame, obsessed with an absent or present man,
blindfolded, crossing two swords, her back to the water.
The truth is, I wake up with lust and loss
and only half believe in something better;
the truth is that I still write twelve-page letters
and blame my acne and my flabby ass
that I am thirty-five and celibate.
Women are lustful and fickle and all alike,
say the hand-laid flower-pressed sheets at the paper-mill.
I pay attention to what lies they tell
us here, but at the flowered lip, hesitate,
one of the tamed girls stopped at the edge to look.

6

One of the tamed girls stopped at the edge to look
at her self in the water, genital self that stains
and stinks, that is synonymous with drains,
wounds, pettiness, stupidity, rebuke.
The pool creates itself, cleansed, puissant, deep
as magma, maker, genetrix. Marie
and I, each with a notebook on her knee,
begin to write, homage the source calls up
or force we find here. There is another source
consecrate in the pool we perch above:

our own intelligent accord that brings
us to the lucid power of the spring
to work at re-inventing work and love.
We may be learning how to tell the truth.

7

We may be learning how to tell the truth.
Distracted by a cinematic sky,
Paris below two dozen shades of grey,
in borrowed rooms we couldn't afford, we both
work over words till we can tell ourselves
what we saw. I get up at eight, go down
to buy fresh croissants, put a saucepan on
and brew first shared coffee. The water solves
itself, salves us. Sideways, hugging the bank,
two stocky women helped each other, drank
from leathery cupped palms. We make our own
descent downstream, getting our shoes wet, care-
fully hoist cold handsful from a crevice where
azure striation swirls beyond the stones.

John Haines

Deserted Cabin

Here in the yellowing
aspen grove,
on Campbell's hill,
the wind is searching
a fallow garden.

I remember the old man
who lived here.
Five years have gone by,
and his house has grown
to resemble his life --
a shallow cave hung
with old hides, rusty
traps and chains,
smelling of eighty years
of unwashed bedding
and rotting harness.

I see him sitting there
now as he used to,
his starved animals gathered
about his bony knees.
He talks to himself
of poverty, cursing softly,
jabbing a stick
at the shadows.

The bitterness of a soul
that wanted only to walk
in the sun, and pick
the ripening berries.

It is like coming home
late in the evening
with a candle in your hand,
and meeting someone
you had forgotten --
the voice is strange.

It is the cold autumn wind
stirring the frozen grass,
as if some life
had just passed there,
bound home
in the early darkness.

Donald Hall

Ox Cart Man

In October of the year,
he counts potatoes dug from the brown field,
counting the seed, counting
the cellar's portion out,
and bags the rest on the cart's floor.

He packs wool sheared in April, honey
in combs, linen, leather
tanned from deerhide,
and vinegar in a barrel
hooped by hand at the forge's fire.

He walks by his ox's head, ten days
to Portsmouth Market, and sells potatoes,
and the bag that carried potatoes,
flaxseed, birch brooms, maple sugar, goose
feathers, yarn.

When the cart is empty he sells the cart.
When the cart is sold he sells the ox,
harness and yoke, and walks
home, his pockets heavy
with the year's coin for salt and taxes,

and at home by fire's light in November cold
stitches new harness
for next year's ox in the barn,
and carves the yoke, and saws planks
building the cart again.

Mark Halperin

Franz Jagesttater's Epistemology

As they argued, the bishop had yelled, *arrogant*
man, furious with Jagesttater who is mounting steps
smoothed by the passage of others. In the courtyard
a swath of light brushes his shoulder. Why
is Berlin so much colder than his Austrian village,
its bluebells and edelweiss? In 1943

the ageless Church holds it is wrong, knowingly,
to serve in an unjust war. Jagesttater's wife,
shifting her chair closer to the fire, hears the cat
yawn who is sleeping where her husband should be
reading to her of oil and grain in the godless east.
Jagesttater's rosary is his single argument: God

gave us reason and meant us to distinguish
good from evil. This is not a man to consider
how long it takes the brain to die and feeling
to shut down, but Jagesttater, shuffling
toward the dark wooden block. He believes in God
and the Holy Catholic Church; he knows this war

is unjust, and trusts his legs will not buckle.
It is sad to die, although belief and trust abide
like the sun clearing the Alps, casting the shadow
of a cross over the play of his small children.
Poor orphans, he permits himself; his gift: belief
in a loving God, and his certainty: *men may know.*

Daniel Halpern

Return

Come back again and again, the fields no
longer hold their colors on limbs of light

over the earth, under the sky, over the soft
dicondra, the clover and weeds that spread,

that pressed their dark root systems into the rich fields.
The old neighbors have passed quietly into the earth.

Your family has broken down and is traveling.
Still, this is where your mouth in humor first closed

over the mouth of the girl who lived behind you,
where you learned to live on the edge of talking.

Come back, the fields are gone and your friends are gone,
the girl behind you has married into another city, the roads

out of town are direct now and fast, and everyone
you knew is gone, or no longer wants to know you.

But you must return, back to the long stretch of main street
reaching across the entire length of the valley,

back to the mild, mid-winter days around Christmas,
back to what is now only remembered because nothing

is the same here anymore. There are no fields, nothing
edible on the land anymore—only the traffic moving

this way, then back again, then back again.
The light is no longer reflected in the earth

but you return because there is always something
that survives: come back again to old friends

living against dark fields, come back again, the family
holding dinner for you, come back, come back again.

Robert Hass

The Origin Of Cities

She is first seen dancing which is a figure
not for art or prayer or the arousal of desire
but for action simply; her breastband is copper,
her crown imitates the city walls. Though she draws us
to her, like a harbor or a rivermouth she sends us away.
A figure of the outward. So the old men grown lazy
in patrician ways lay out cash for adventures.
Imagining a rich return, they buy futures
and their slaves haunt the waterfront for news of ships.
The young come from the villages dreaming.
Pleasure and power draw them. They are employed
to make inventories and grow very clever,
multiplying in their heads, deft at the use of letters.
When they are bored, they write down old songs from the villages,
and the cleverest make new songs in the old forms
describing the pleasures of the city, their mistresses,
old shepherds and simpler times. And the temple
where the farmer grandfathers of the great merchants worshipped,
the dim temple across from the marketplace
which was once a stone altar in a clearing in the forest,
where the nightwatch pisses now against a column in the moonlight,
is holy to them; the wheat mother their goddess of sweaty sheets,
of what is left in the air when that glimpsed beauty
turns the corner, of love's punishment and the wracking
of desire. They make songs about that. They tell
stories of heroes and brilliant lust among the gods.
These are amusements. She dances, the ships go forth,
slaves and peasants labor in the fields, maimed soldiers
ape monkeys for coins outside the wineshops,
the craftsmen work in bronze and gold, accounts
are kept carefully, what goes out, what returns.

William Heyen

Redwings

Maybe you've noticed that around here
red-winged blackbirds aren't rare,
but aren't seen often, either, and then, at distance,
banking away from roads as we pass.

But one morning, I saw a hundred,
more, feeding on seed I'd spread
under a line of pines planted
more than a hundred years before.

Almost at rest, their feathers folded close,
only their yellow wingbars
break their black bodies. But when, as they did,
all at once, they lifted, that *red* . . .

I've tried for a long time, and maybe should,
to tell you how the disembodied redwings
flared and vanished.
I've lost them in every telling.

So much for me. I could die now, anyway.
Could you? We will close our eyes
and rest, in case the blackbirds, in slow
motion, assume the flames they are, and rise.

Jim Heynen

Morning Chores

In my bed I turned toward light
and the odor of work on my hands,
toward the moist clothes on the floor
with the barnyard still breathing in them.
Outside the chorus began:
roosters crowing, dogs barking,
but I was not sure of the dawn
until I heard myself calling the cows.
Dew collected on my shoes,
pigs rose from wet earth,
milk dripped from the udders of cows.
Everywhere the fresh urge of morning
led us into our story.
The cows ate from my hands,
the milk flowed from my hands.
What happened between, I didn't know
and didn't care. It was enough.

Today all I hear is that memory
as I rise in this suburban light,
knowing too well I am here:
my hands full of dishes, a bed
with two cats and a wife
whose love sinks with me in yearning
for the small voice we all leave brawling
in one lost field or another.

Still the residing light
for us who have lived among animals
is like a religion that stands
when the old church crumbles.
For to have moved with the beasts who know
something more than reason or law
but who accept the sun in the morning
and the hands that feed them
is to have been the voice in a song
that no one is singing,
happier than one who praises
and knows he is praising.

Even now I can feel
as the city untangles around me
that constant flow in the earth
that wants to be glad.
And I offer no more than I can
from a life that was fed among animals,
what follows me now in my going,
a dawn that never stops breaking.

George Hitchcock

When I Came Back to Dancing Misery

when I came back to the stuffed dragonfly
when I came back to the lame left foot of salt
when I came back to the fluttering ventricle
            and the map of polar crutches

I saw the stones of undone kilometers
I saw embrocations of jellied petrol
I saw the sofas made of icebound topsoil
            and the map of crosses

the blowflies land on the earlobe
the blowlfies land on blossoms of bone
the blowflies leave their boiling gloves
            on the manes of diagonal horses

I lick the piss-stained snow from my fingers
I lick the porkfat from bloated knuckles
I lick red tears from still another sunset
            on the map of roses

when I came back to dancing misery
when I came back to explosive sequins
when I came back to the hems of warfare
            and the map of my burning bridges

the strawberry grew in the lunar trenches
the strawberry grew in the afternoon's antlers
the strawberry grew on the captain's laughter
            and the map of losses

Daniel Hoffman

On The Industrial Highway

Approaching the Walt
Whitman Bridge you pass
an affluent world --

a subculture of spouts,
nozzles, ducts, a host
of snakes and ladders

in nests and thickets
or by tribes, laying
dinosaur farts

against the sun.
I drive slowly through the
stink and gawk at

shapes that no
familiarity breeds,
a ghostless city

called 'gas works,' never
meant for death or living.
A pipe pulses

flame in secret
code on the gashed sky.
Here are things

whose archetypes
have not yet been dreamed.
There's no more perfect

duct than these
ducts, pipes, facts
burdened with nothing

anticipating
unhappened memories,
visionary things.

Richard Hugo

Glen Uig

Believe in this couple this day who come
to picnic in the Faery Glen. They pay rain
no matter, or wind. They spread their picnic
under a gale-stunted rowan. Believe they grew tired
of giants and heroes and know they believe
in wise tiny creatures who live under the rocks.

Believe these odd mounds, the geologic joke
played by those wise tiny creatures far from
the world's pitiful demands: make money, stay sane.
Believe the couple, by now soaked to the skin,
sing their day as if dry, as if sheltered inside
Castle Ewen. Be glad Castle Ewen's only a rock
that looks like a castle. Be glad for no real king.

These wise tiny creatures, you'd better believe,
have lived through it all: the Viking occupation,
clan torturing clan, the Clearances, the World War
II bomber gone down, a fiery boom
on Beinn Edra. They saw it from here. They heard
the sobs of last century's crofters trail off below
where every day the Conon sets out determined for Uig.
They remember the Viking who wandered off course,
under the hazelnut tree hating aloud all he'd done.

Some days dance in the bracken. Some days go out
wide and warm on bad roads to collect the dispossessed
and offer them homes. Some days celebrate addicts
sweet in their dreams and hope to share with them
a personal spectrum. The loch here's only a pond,
the monster in it small as a wren.

Believe the couple who have finished their picnic
and make wet love in the grass, the wise tiny creatures
cheering them on. Believe in milestones, the day
you left home forever and the cold open way
a world wouldn't let you come in. Believe you
and I are that couple. Believe you and I sing tiny
and wise and could if we had to eat stone and go on.

David Ignatow

My Own House

As I view the leaf my theme is not the shades of meaning that the
mind conveys of it but my desire to make the leaf speak to tell me,
Chlorophyll, chlorophyll, breathlessly, and I would rejoice with it
and in turn would reply, Blood, and the leaf nod. Having spoken to
each other, we would find our topics inexhaustible and, imagine,
as I grow old and the leaf begins to fade and turn brown, the
thought of being buried in the ground would become so familiar to
me, so thoroughly known to me through conversation with the leaf,
that my walk among the trees, after completing this poem would be
like entering my own house.

Laura Jensen

Household

Grudges mend and wear and turn in winter
but they turn again, astounded
if the wish has not been made,
nor the stars considered,
nor time kept useful in absence.

These are the needles.
They are not thrown down
when they are stubborn.

But a fingertip is sleeping in a thimble.
There is a haystack of needles
leaving every farm with the country daughter,
needles spending their lives now
forgotten from raincoats in a rush,
shaking from cuffs and emptying from shoes.

It is not easy to sew with an ignorant needle.

Once building a needle, once building a weed
was a young time, once, that leaves itself be
a wheedling eye, a thread of light
between pins and the reputable grasses,
their brass teasing eyes to believe.

If there were no troubles, borrowing,
the troubles would be in the rivers
and the rivers would be rivers
that the troubled find.

The lake is rising like an argyle sock
on a darning egg grown wings.
And even with everything there would be
the fear, the warning, and the needles
looking down at my knees from my mind.
The needles close up in their packets
as they are remembered, what the feminine
should have kept in their lives,
so many eyes and only one authority of paper.

Don Johnson

The Children's Hour

Not falling
but curling up
out of oak woods
at the lawn's edge,
summer darkness
is flooding our yard
like the tide.
The grass dampens,
washes away.
The last glowing buds
of the flame azalea
go out. The black Lab,
Midnight, disappears.

Bare to the waist,
the children are fauns,
their animal haunches
blanketed
in dark.

The older one
bends for a stick
and is gone,
and for a moment
the younger
is only
the luminous movement
of hands
about a face
half-eclipsed
in shadow.

Here on this porch
like a prow
the evening laps
at my feet.
I hear the last-
washed glass
chime from the kitchen.
I am struck
by the almost-
audible ticking
of fireflies.

Donald Justice

Thinking about the Past

Certain moments will never change, nor stop being—
My mother's face all smiles, all wrinkles soon;
The rock wall building, built, collapsed then, fallen;
Our upright loosening downward slowly out of tune—
All fixed into place now, all rhyming with each other.
That red-haired girl with wide mouth—Eleanor—
Forgotten thirty years—her freckled shoulders, hands,
The breast of Mary Something, freed from a white swimsuit,
Damp, sandy, warm; or Margery's, a small,caught bird—
Darkness they rise from, darkness they sink back toward.
O marvellous early cigarettes! O bitter smoke, Benton...
And Kenny in wartime whites, crisp, cocky,
Time a bow bent with his certain failure.
Dusks, dawns; waves; the ends of songs...

Ode

Old tumbril rolling with me till I die,
Divided face I'm hung with, hindside-to,
How can a peace be drawn between us, who
    Never see eye to eye?

Why, when it seems I speak straight from the heart
Most solemn thought, do you too have to speak,
Let out a horselaugh, whistle as I break
    The news to Mother that I must depart?

Moon always waxing full, barrage balloon,
Vesuvius upside down, dual rump roast,
Cave of the Winds, my Mississippi coast,
    Cyclops forever picking up and chucking stone,

Caboose, poor ass I'm saddled with from birth,
Without your act, the dirty deed I share,
How could the stuck-up spirit in me bear
    Coming back down to earth?

Faye Kicknosway

from **Janie**

An eye, a viscous eye, with the sight stopped and nothing in the
eyehole. And the nothing grows. And sometimes it hatches out of
the belly and against the will of the belly. With pigeon feet and
a beak with snot at its corners. Into the belly of a room and the
belly of a family. It rises up and reaches out, first with its
head and its shoulders and last with its sex and its legs and feet.
It won't die; it won't come loose, it will grow and it will be out-
side, only it will be dark and watery. If the sun comes into the
room where it sits, it will be transparent as sweat. It will glow
and the outline of the chair will be seen through its body. It
will catch in the eye. There will be no movement except from the
pigeon on the windowledge picking at its feathers.
"The pigeons, Ma; look at the pigeons." One voice becoming another
voice. The room at the back of the brain where the figure comes to
sit, catches at the edges of the tongue as though it were a hand.
Catches and fills the tongue with its speech. And the pigeons, they
are lovers, coming first to the window and then into the window and
then to the female body and then into the female body. "Look
at the pigeons." Their noise is the noise of a belly growing, the
walls of the room coming loose because of the visitation. The eye
at the side of the head is red and the size of the ceiling. Listen,
the eye at the side of the head makes a noise as it blinks, a noise
like airplane propellers, like razors tied to strings from a fan and
slicing at the summer air. Pigeon feet rising up and reaching out,
first as though they were faces--they are faces, dream faces, leaf
faces, pod faces, faces soaked in vinegar and wrapped in newspapers
to preserve them. Body the shade, the place where the feathers fold
closed.
The walls sweat. The mouth is useless and so is the tongue. The
noise of the trees and the stairs and the toilet speak more clearly.
The voice in the room in the brain comes through the brain's neon
tubing. The words are an electric cross blinking. Blinking the way
the body blinks when it has had a visitation, when angels have come
to the window and come in through the window and come to the body
and in through the body. Openings
are not necessary. Eyes and lips are not necessary. The body is
a hole, a passage between containers. Rain, sweat, coffee. The
body is a sponge,a dipper, a water tap. The sky blinks, the room
and the body in the room blink, lose the image and have to create
another to replace it.

Peter Klappert

Estienne
　　　　(Paris, 1939)

I
　　　　No matter who is using the body
I return to the scene of the crime,
and like a narrative of the grave, the plot
lacks complication.
　　　　　　　　　I have kicked
away my shoes and bitten a cushion.
My arm becomes a stranger
standing in the room, unbuttoning,
leaving a skin of trousers on the floor.
His hand goes for the light and in the dark
I know again the brief, unutterable
perfume of the stick the sack the cup
and the pillar thrilling into my hand.
With the lids of my eyes half-drawn, I see
most clearly: it is one whose name I never knew,
one, perhaps, whose figure, back-lighted
by a mist of stars, had seemed
translucent as a letter from a lover.
Oh, he may have been no more than a yegg
or a gunsel, and our pause together
a gooseberry lay--but *this* is my striptease,
and when I give the air my mouth
I can taste what he is saying.
　　　　　　　　　　　Then the clock
comes back, the face that never changes,
the old reproof. On my elbows I lean
and stare across the bed
into a land of shadows in the mirror.
And I go to the sink like Pilate.

II
　　　　　　　　　　　　--which by a sudden perversity
reminds me of a few syllables by Estienne,
my former friend the poet
who came late. We were buttoning up
at la Place de la Bastille, just after a manifestation,
on a night so overcast
you could see clear to the bottom of heartache.

　　Open the trees! (he cried) *Take out*
　　　　the stars that nail the barricade of night!
　　The wind has flung its chiffon
　　　　across the blood in the cheeks of the moon

and under the wings of the night-heron
small frightened things are singing
to keep up courage.
O all the dark
sons of the waterways have poled their wicker boats
out over the deep clear currents...

Well, I suggested,
no baboon ever took singing lessons
and no bird needs to. But why do you write
for the bankrupt past? He replied
that he would know joy
and must compose in a dead language.

III

Poor Estienne--his eyes
already swam like two albino goldfish in his glasses
and his wide thin shoulders hung
about him like a carapace. But in Annus Miribilis
1934, he still had two lips
and a sweet tongue to curl between them.

"This age (he used to say) will get
its politics from a chanteuse
and its beliefs from a brush salesman.
It takes its calendar from Judas
who went out and hanged himself."

"The soul in flight
from its own history (I countered)
and the body aerodynamically unsound.
But there's another version to that story
--here, let me give you a hand with those buttons--
which says every eachman
gives to Death his name. Which is to say
we come like dummies with titles on our spines
and each by whatever talent
writes his own penny-dreadful.
Few are eloquent
though many loquacious, and fewer still
compose a Senecan death."

"By which is meant 'terse suicide'?"

"More rare than Mary Tofts
giving birth to bunnies.
                    One should perhaps
keep scribbling for the censor."

"You omit the exhibitionists," he cried
(snapping his buttons open with a vengeance),
"Peregrinus before the Olympic roar
reclining perfumed on his pyre, and Petronius
doing and undoing his veins among his friends... "

                    "--whose lips, we imagine,
spoke like lilies to his pleasure!
Funerals may be cheap theatre, Estienne,
but a concert without encores
is a poor bargain."

IV
"My dear Matthew, I can't go on
writing words my tongue refuses to caress.
My knees keep walking, my feet are lifeless,
and a creature devoid of understanding
pursues me in sorrow. Forever
we walk forward toward ourselves,
but can one speak of death
when there is nothing left to bury?"

        "And are the dead named, Estienne?
        Or do we go to the majority anonymous?
        The dead would like to know."

V
Ah, Estienne. There you were
already measured for wooden pyjamas and going off
in ten minutes to be
the space one walks through where a friend has stood.
And we both heard your Black Maria
making her frantic bleat in la Rue de la Paix.

        "No," you said at last, "I'm shut of that.
        Images of smashing glass, of a descent
        from a dark building to darker street,
        of swimming too far out.
                            We know the world
        will rise again in April
        in all its glorious redundancy,

but it rises for us only
if we fight the world all winter,
for *we* are April's precondition.
                              Light,
the only light comes from each man
rubbing against the darkness,
though a soft and sulphurous match
that man might be.
                         I'm not clear what I
can do about God.
Try not to hurt Him, I think, stay alive,
I think, in His rare and expensive sunlight."

Yes, and one other thing, Estienne.
After confession but before absolution,
try to dare to remember to say

                    "Je te remercie."

Bill Knott

Streetcorner

The wind blows a piece of paper to my feet.
I pick it up.
It is not a petition for my death.

Maxine Kumin

Halfway

As true as I was born into
my mother's bed in Germantown,
the gambrel house in which I grew
stood halfway up a hill, or down,
between a convent and a madhouse.

The nunnery was white and brown.
In summertime they said the mass
on a side porch, from rocking chairs.
The priest came early on the grass,
black in black rubbers up the stairs
or have I got it wrong? The mass
was from the madhouse and the priest
came with a black bag to his class
and ministered who loved him least.
They shrieked because his needles stung.
They sang for Christ upon his cross.
The plainsong and the bedlam hung
on the air and blew across
into the garden where I played.

I saw the sisters' linens flap
on the clothesline while they prayed,
and heard them tell their beads and slap
their injuries. But I have got
the gardens mixed. It must have been
the mad ones who cried out to blot
the frightened sinner from his sin.
The nuns were kind. They gave me cake
and told me lives of saints who died
aflame and silent at the stake
and when I saw their Christ, I cried

where I was born, where I outgrew
my mother's bed in Germantown.
All the iron truths I knew
stood halfway up a hill, or down.

Philip Levine

The Voice

Small blue flowers like points
of sky were planted to pin
the earth above me, and still
I went on reaching through leaf
and grass blade and the saw-toothed
arms of thistles for the sky
that dozed above my death.
When the first winter came
I slept and wakened in late March
to hear the flooded fields
singing their hymns to the birds.
The birds returned. And so it was
that I began to learn what changes
I had undergone. Not as in
a sea change had I been pared
down to the white essential
bones, nor did I remain huddled
around the silence after the breath
stormed and collapsed. I was large,
at first a meadow where wild
mustard quivered in warm winds.
Then I slipped effortlessly up
the foothills overlooking
that great awakening valley.
Then it seemed I was neither
the valley below or the peaks above
but a great breathing silence
that turned slowly through darkness
and light, which were the same,
toward darkness and light. I
remember the first time I spoke
in a human voice. I had been
sweeping away the last of sunset
in a small rural town, and I
passed shuddering through a woman
on her solitary way home, her arms
loaded with groceries. She said,
Oh my God! as though she were
lost and frightened, and so I let
the light linger until she found
her door. In truth for a while
I was scared of myself, even
my name scared me, for that's
what I'd been taught, but in
a single round of seasons I saw
no harm could come from me, and now
I embrace whatever pleases me,
and the earth is my one home,

as it always was, the earth
and perhaps some day the sky too
and all the climbing things between.

Larry Levis

Blue Stones

> *for my son, Nicholas*

I suspect
They will slide me into a cold bed,
A bed that has been brought in,
Out of the night
And past the fraying brick of the warehouse,
Where maybe a workman took an afternoon nap,
And woke staring up
At what sky he could see through one window.
But if he kept staring,
And thought that the bed took its gray color
From the sky, and kept watching that sky
Even after he had finished his cigarette,
He might learn
How things outlive us.
And maybe he would be reminded that the body, too,
Is only a thing, a joke it kept trying to tell us,
And now the moment for hearing it
Is past.
All I will have to decide, then,
Is how to behave during
Those last weeks, when the drawers
Of the dresser remain closed,
And the mirror is calm, and reflects nothing,
And outside, tangled
In the hard branches,
The moon appears.
I see how poor it is,
How it owns nothing.
I look at it a long time, until
I feel empty, as if I had travelled on foot
For three days, and become simple,
The way light was simple on the backs
Of horses as my father approached them,
Quietly, with a bridle.
My father thought dying
Was like standing trial for crimes
You could not remember.
Then someone really does throw
The first stone.
It is blue,
And seems to be made of the sky itself.
The breath goes out of you.
Tonight, the smoke holds still
Against the hills and trees outside this town,
And there is no hope
Of acquittal.

*

But *you*? Little believer, little
Straight, unbroken, and tireless thing,
Someday, when you are twenty-four and walking through
The streets of a foreign city, Stockholm
Or Trieste,
Let me go with you a little way,
Let me be that stranger you won't notice,
And when you turn and enter a bar full of young men
And women, and your laughter rises,
Like the stones of a path up a mountain,
To say that no one has died,
I promise I will not follow.
I will cross at the corner in my gray sweater.
I will not have touched you,
As I did, for so many years,
On the hair and the left shoulder.
I will silence my hand that wanted to.
I will put it in my pocket, and let it clutch
The cold, blue stones they give you,
After you have lived.

Laurence Lieberman

God's Measurements
(Todaiji Temple, Nara)

> *The statue weighs 452 tons, measures 53.5 ft. in height and has a*
> *face 16 ft. long by 9.5 ft. wide, eyes 3.9 ft. wide, a nose 1.6 ft. high,*
> *a mouth 3.7 ft. wide, ears 8.5 ft. long, hands 6.8 ft. long, and thumbs*
> *4.8 ft. long. The materials employed are estimated as follows: 437*
> *tons of bronze; 165 lbs. of mercury; 288 lbs. of pure gold; 7 tons of*
> *vegetable wax; and an amazing amount of charcoal and other materials.*
> > *—Japan: The Official Guide*

As incense smoke thins, a stupendous,
     wide, brooding face emerges above us. The long
         ribbon-looped
ears, ending in weighty teardrop-
     fat lobes, slowly unravel from the wrappings of smoke
       trails
     as we advance, the whole bronze olive-green head
       mushrooming from its mask
         of mist. It floats, hovers—balloonlike, isolate—
     over the befogged shoulders. A cosmos
        of global body,
           seated cross-legged on a great lotus-
           blossom bronze pedestal, ascends

into the clearing before us,
     the pedestal in turn installed on a broader stone base
which knows touch of our hastily donned
     slippers, blocking our passage. Not one forward step
       possible,
     we backstep twice to see the more clearly
        over the jutting head-
          high edge of stone, the full figure now vivid
       and preternaturally clear before us,
         body draped in swirls
           of cloud, itself cloud-shaped, cloud-alloyed,
           growing into a mass, a solid—

if wavery—form. Still, it is the head,
     so distant, holds us. Why do we so thrill at eye-guessed
estimates of measurements, measurements!
     The eyes and mouth, wide as you are long, my son;
       the length
    of ears makes two of you, the height of lofty face
       three of me, and, yes,
         you could ride lying on the thumb, your near mate
      for length and width, the two of you nestled
        together mimicking
            a God's freakish double thumb! But, no, I
           will not lift you to the stone ledge,

launching your unstoppable climb
to test my twin-thumbs caprice, despite your scandalous
wails
reverberating in the temple
upper chambers, strident in my ears; nor shall I scold
or muzzle you, but hoist you to my shoulders,
where, first clasping hands
for lift and support as you unfold to your full
height above my head, I clench your ankles,
as much to steady
and balance you as to prevent surprise
leaps. Together, of a tallness

to match, or exceed, the whole hand's length,
let us promenade around His Excellency's right flank.
Now, wobblingly, we stalk: you, stilt-jack,
in love with instant towers sprung from the idiot body's
endlessly stretchable elastic of flesh, I
half scaffold, half anchor,
the two of us a father-son hobbling hinge—
telescope of our bones, joined end to end,
not doubled up
in laughter or loss of balance but bending
and unbending into beatitudes....

We look up, to scrutinize the God, stilt-
walking our charmed gavotte. Then, looking into
each other's eyes—
I staring up, you staring down—
we both shudder, communing between your flexed legs,
spread
the width of my two shoulders: our four eyes,
riveted in silence,
agree! We have seen the bronze head nod. The
eyelids
flutter. The bronze bosom draw breath. The tarnished
skins
of metal wrinkling
into folds over charcoal hid ribs. Organs—
heart and lungs— of vegetable wax, waxen

liver, waxen pancreas. All glands,
mercury, but in pure form, not poisons fed upon
by dying
fish hordes. Our eyes swear we both saw
bronze flesh breathe, bronze knees shift for comfort
under all
that obese weight (no gold in the fat buttocks, fat

hips, we agree to that!),
grand flab he can never jog off in throes
of deep meditation. Does he diet, or fast?
Does he shed bronze, gold,
or weightless, sad wax only? We crane our
necks
to see how he leans and sways, as we wend

our wide, counterclockwise, happy circle
around him, counting splendid curled petals of the
great lotus-
blossom seat, the petals alternately
pointing upward and curving downward, the puffed
whirlwinds
of incense smoke eddying up, thinning out,
in sudden gusts and lulls,
as if the blossom itself exhaled the perfume
clouds submerging all but the Ancient's head, breath
after vaporous breath...
We revolve, degree by slow degree, circling
the statue's base, half again wider

than the vast lotus throne half again
the diameter of the bloated God's girth, and
we behold
the thousand views of the Buddha's
changing postures, the torso's bulk crafted by an army
of master sculptors. *Eight near-perfect castings*
in three years. Aborted casts,
unnumbered. No surmising how many dozens
of failed castings, cracked one-hundred-foot-wide
molds, collapsed scaffolds,
casters of irreplaceable genius crushed
in falling debris... Sudden glare!

We squint, sun cascading into the hall
from hidden windows high in the temple cupola—
thousands
of sparkly points on the statue's
coruscating skull flare on, off, on, off, and I can see
great circles connecting all dots of light
on meticulously shaped
rondures of annealed jaw plates, shoulder plates,
breast
plates, my sight travelling in arcs and swirls, curved
lines running in a mesh
of intersecting spirals dense as cross-
hatching in the divinely crafted

anatomies of Hieronymus Bosch
       or the woodcut body dissections of Vesalius: God's
or human's, all the light-lines engraved
    on the celestial body's grandly continuous surface
    intersect. *Our body, a wing shining*
       in the happy, happy
          light of its wholeness. A moonlit angel's wing
      in flight. Or underwater devil ray's
        wing torchlit
            by diver's forehead searchlight beam...
            High throne-back behind the Buddha's

head usurps our view while we wind
    around his back side, topped not by headrest or
      flat cushion,
as it had appeared to us wrongly
    in profile, but a goldleaf-covered broad wooden halo
    decorated with portraits of sixteen Bosatsu,
      by our ambulatory
        count, a troop of gilt sub-deities, satellites
    in orbit perpetually— each a mirror,
      or reflecting moon,
          to the one Daibutsu...*Oh, look! The*
          whole halo
        is shimmering, dancing before our eyes!

Thomas Lux

Graveyard by the Sea

I wonder if they sleep better here
so close to the elemental pentameter
of the sea which comes in incessantly?
Just a few square acres of sand
studded mainly with thick posts—
as if the coffins beneath were boats
tied fast to prevent further drift.
I half stumble around one pre-dawn,
just a dog following the footprints
of another dog with me, and stop

before one particular grave: a cross
inlaid with large splinters of mirror.
Whoever lies here is distinguished,
certainly, but I wonder—why mirrors?
For signaling? Who? No, they're embedded
in the stone and so can't be flicked
to reflect the sun or moonlight.
Is the sleeper here unusually vain
and the glass set for those times of dark
ascensions — to smooth the death gown,

to apply a little lipstick to the white
worms of the lips? No again. I think
they're for me and the ones who come,
like me, at this hour, in this half-light.
The ones who come half-drunk, half-wild,
and wholly in fear— so we may gaze
into the ghosts of our own faces,
and be touched by this chill of all
chills— and then go home, alive,
to sleep the sleep of the awake. . . .

William Matthews

A Late Movie

On Haiti two years ago he stalled
to a coma and his wife learned
a little voodoo to lure him out.
Since then he's noticed nothing strange
in her except those usual opacities
a husband or wife flies through:
clouds, the weather of others.

Meanwhile she's been burning dried
spiders, etc., and when he discovers her
silly paraphenalia he's happy
to be adamant. Maybe he's seen
something odd in her after all
and is glad to think this is it.

But it wasn't just duff he made her
throw away, nor only the litter
on which decay lies down its bed -
burning body, it was a system
of details, and so a sort of memory.

Whatever it was she's sick without it
and wherever they fall his feet are wrong
and sound to him like heartbeats.
He can hear the space between them grow
and then he can see it, a sift
in which the swindle and swell
of matter shine, the way salt glowed
in the oceans he dreamed as a boy,
as if the stars were underwater.

His wife's fevers flurry and subside.
She might as well be underwater.
He tries to hold her. His arms waver
and bend. Not that he believes her magic
now, but that his is little but burning
ashes, burning water, burning smoke.
Love might ask anything of you.
Or fire might ask anything of you
and say that its name is love.

Mekeel McBride

The Will To Live

On the green lawn of a city park
a sentence of dark insects completes itself:

Believe! Believe!
Above, two Monarchs matter and flash

in this immense summer air.
Small scraps of wing, good weather, a will

to live, they come
from the tenuous country of now

whatever the heart is asking for. Even if I
weren't here

they'd still congratulate the sky
with a fragile disbelief in sorrow. Graceful

as the hands of the deaf
they form a language in air that I understand

almost not at all. Being human
I might say

they kiss and part and kiss again but
know they're governed by desire

or law or lack of these
beyond me. They fling themselves

against a sky so big
they do not understand it's there. Clouds

fat and ample, grow
fatter still and if the old June maples

stand weighted and without words
it is not from human grief, or any other.

Heather McHugh

Retired School-Teacher

Brilliant planets float in that black lake.
She is losing her vision.
Her pupils are old.
All night long she stays up
trying to remember
an animal from the past,
imaginary, made
to swim in sight, to burn in tears,
to turn the heavens and the seas around.

On the coast of her youth
light-years away she loved
to let the waves come over her.
She talks some sense into herself.
Sleep, sleep. It is much too late
for children. That sinks in.

Deep in the dream and far
from all attachment she feels

the first of the star-fish touch.

His Body

He doesn't like it, of course -
Others, who don't wear it but see it, do.
He's pale, like a big desert, but you can find flowers.
No, not entirely pale:
Between shin and ankle the twin sun marks;
And where his shirt (now draped from a chair back)
Was, he contrasts with dark hands
And neck/face
Like a rained-on street where a car has just been driven
Away.
Don't picture a beer paunch.
And he is a smooth animal, or soft where he isn't smooth,
Down to his toadskin testicles.
He lies prone on clean bedsheets.
There is a single light in the room.
Now run your hand down his back, its small, and up
The hips and over. Their sheen's like that
On blue metal music boxes made to hold powder.
But the rest of him is sprouted with black down-going hair,
His whiskers in so many foxholes,
Eager to out.
Are they in any order?
Age has so far
Remained locked inside.
I'm not a doctor
And glad not to have a doctor's viewpoint.
I'm glad I haven't the petite,
Overwhelmed sight of an antibody.
And yet I'm not just anybody perusing his body -
I have a reason to like it better than I like other bodies.
Someone else can praise those,
Each lonely and earthly, wanting to be celestial.

William Meredith

Examples of Created Systems

for Robert Penn Warren

i. the stars

We look out at them on clear nights, thrilled
rather than comforted -- brilliance and
distance put us in mind of our
own burnings and losses. And then who
flung them there, in a sowing motion
suggesting that random is beautiful?

ii. archipelagoes

Or again, the islands that the old
cartographers, triangulating
their first glimpses of bays and peaks, set
down, and which the rich traveller, from
a high winter chair, chooses among
today -- chains of jade thrown across the
torso of the sea-mother, herself
casually composed.

iii. work camps and prisons

　　　　　　　The homeless
Solzhenitsyn, looking at Russia,
saw a configuration of camps
spotting his homeland, 'ports' where men
and women were forced to act out
the birth-throes of volcanic islands,
the coral patience of reefs, before
a 'ship', a prison train, bore them down
that terrible archipelago
conceived and made by men like ourselves.

iv. those we love

Incorrigibly (it is our nature)
when we look at a map we look for
the towns and valleys and waterways
where loved people constellate, some of
them from our blood, some from our own loins.
This fair scattering of matter is
all we will know of creation, at
first hand. We flung it there, in a learned
gesture of sowing -- random, lovely.

James Merrill

Page From The Koran

A small vellum environment
Overrun with black
Scorpions of Kufic script-- their ranks
All trigger tail and gold vowel-sac--
At auction this mild winter morning went
For six hundred Swiss francs.

By noon, fire from the same blue heavens
Had half erased Beirut.
Allah be praised, it said on crude handbills,
For guns and Nazarenes to shoot.
"How gladly with proper words," said Wallace Stevens,
"The soldier dies." Or kills.

God's very word, then, stung the heart
To greed and rancor? Yet
Not where its last glow touches one spare man
Inked-in against his minaret
--Letters so handled they are life, and hurt,
Leaving the scribe immune?

W.S. Merwin

To Dana For Her Birthday

Something continues and   I don't know what to call it
though the language is full of suggestions
in the way of language
                                            but they are all anonymous
and it's almost your birthday   music next to my bones

these nights we hear the horses   running in the rain
it stops and the moon comes out   and we are still here
the leaks in the roof go on dripping   after the rain has passed
smell of ginger flowers   slips through the dark house
down near the sea   the slow heart of the beacon flashes

the long way to you is still tied to me   but it brought me to you
I keep wanting to give you   what is already yours
it is the morning   of the mornings together
breath of summer   oh my found one
the sleep in the same current   and each waking to you

when I open my eyes   you are what I wanted to see

Robert Morgan

Mirror Farming

In the colder climates they
ricochet and double
the solarity by
paving the soil with white rocks,
or even, in the rainy northern isles,
backlighting each plant with cloth
or mirrors like summer snow
to multiply the stingy heat.
The vegetables accept and nourish on
that theater, feeding at
the compound star
and adjusting leaves to blot the crossfire.
New tropisms mature in the long
crystal of day,
finding space attentive, fertile,
a hover of suns
as the sheets and pages
gather near at hand
distant chaoses, fusions.

Howard Moss

The Long Island Night

Nothing as miserable has happened before.
The Long Island night has refused its moon.
La belle dame sans merci's next door.
The Prince of Darkness is on the phone.

Certain famous phrases of our time
Have taken on the glitter of poems,
Like "Catch me before I kill again,"
And "Why are you sitting in the dark alone?'

Lisel Mueller

The Blind Leading The Blind

Take my hand. There are two of us in this cave.
The sound you hear is water; you will hear it forever.
The ground you walk on is rock. I have been here before.
People come here to be born, to discover, to kiss,
to dream and to dig and to kill. Watch for the mud.
Summer blows in with scent of horses and roses;
fall with the sound of sound breaking; winter shoves
its empty sleeve down the dark of your throat.
You will learn toads from diamonds, the fist from the palm,
love from the sweat of love, falling from flying.
There are a thousand turnoffs. I have been here before.
Once I fell off a precipice. Once I found gold.
Once I stumbled on murder, the thin parts of a girl.
Walk on, keep walking, there are axes above us.
Watch for occasional bits and bubbles of light -
birthdays for you, recognitions: *yourself, another.*
Watch for the mud. Listen for bells, for beggars.
Something with wings went crazy against my chest once.
There are two of us here. Touch me.

Carol Muske

The Invention of Cuisine

Imagine for a moment
the still life of our meals,
meat followed by yellow cheese,
grapes pale against the blue armor of fish.

Imagine a thin woman
before bread was invented,
playing a harp of wheat in the fields.
There is a stone, and behind her
the bones of the last killed,
the black bird on her shoulder
that a century later
will fly with trained and murderous intent.

They are not very hungry
because cuisine has not yet been invented.
Nor has falconry,
nor the science of imagination.

All they have is the pure impulse to eat,
which is not enough to keep them alive
and this little moment
before the woman redeems
the sprouted seeds at her feet
and gathers the olives falling from the trees
for her recipes.

Imagine. Out in the fields
this very moment
they are rolling the apples to press,
the lamb turns in a regular aura of smoke.

See, the woman looks once behind her
before picking up the stone,
looks back once at the edible beasts,
the edible trees,
that clean digestible sky
above the white stream
where small creatures live and die
looking upon each other
as food.

Jack Myers

Winging It

> *They try having each other without pain,*
> *try sparing each other the embarrassment*
> *of lifting an empty glass to drink,*
> *of reaching for a hand that's moved,*
> *of having to part by the clock, unhealed*
> *and throbbing against their clothes.*
> *   -Barbara Orlovsky*

You and the woman under you
shove off behind closed eyes
and say in unison, "Take me there."

It looks awkward --
two different wings
fused against a great idea.

But the opening of this gift
is half the gift.
The rest is light, a flash

that slows the most delicate gesture
to a roar which pulses out
like ripples in a pond
and moves the stars a little.

                    *

Ever since I was born
there's been an angel tumbling to earth.
One wing has landed in a tree
though it looks like a bird
has torn itself free
and taken off.

Either I'm invincible
or something in me has given up.

                    *

Under the crackle and blare
my woman whispers, "What is it?"
And I find myself for no reason
saying, "Don't bother. Don't ask."

What is the question?

We are fire tearing from fire
and, reassured, we veer away.

*

All those years I took
the whitened crying of the mind
for silence.

Then what did I hear?

I want to blow out the sun and drift awhile,
for sometimes darkness is a mirror
you can walk into and, turning around,
light up the world.

From here middle age is a wilderness
which looks exactly like the world.

Howard Nemerov

The Tapestry

On this side of the tapestry
There sits the bearded king,
And round about him stand
His lords and ladies in a ring.
His hunting dogs are there,
And armed men at command.

On that side of the tapestry
The formal court is gone,
The kingdom is unknown;
Nothing but thread to see,
Knotted and rooted thread
Spelling a world unsaid.

Men do not find their ways
Through a seamless maze,
And all direction lose
In a labyrinth of clues,
A forest of loose ends
Where sewing never mends.

John Frederick Nims

The Young Ionia

If you could come on the late train for
      The same walk
Or a hushed talk by the fireplace
      When the ash flares
As a heart could (if a heart would) to
      Recall you,
To recall all in a long
      Look, to enwrap you
As it once had when the rain streamed on the
      Fall air,
And we knew, then, it was all wrong,
      It was love lost
And a year lost of the few years we
      Account most —
But the bough blew and the cloud
      Blew and the sky fell
From its rose ledge on the wood's rim to
      The wan brook,
And the clock read to the half-dead
      A profound page
As the cloud broke and the moon spoke and the
      Door shook —

If you could come, and it meant come at the
      Steep price
We regret yet as the debt swells
      In the nighttime
And the *could come, if you could* hum in
      The skull's drum
And the limbs writhe till the bed
      Cries like a hurt thing —
If you could — ah but the moon's dead and the
      Clock's dead.
For we know now: we can give all
      But it won't do,
Not the day's length nor the black strength nor
      The blood's flush.
What we took once for a sure thing,
      For delight's right,
For the clear eve with its wild star in
      The sunset,
We would have back at the old
      Cost, at the old grief
And we beg love for the same pain — for a
      Last chance!
Then the god turns with a low

Laugh (as the leaves hush)
But the eyes ice and there's no twice: the
    Benign gaze
Upon some woe but on ours no.
    And the leaves rush.

Carole Oles

Francestown Suite

for Jabez Holmes, d. May 11, 1824,
Francestown, New Hampshire

Nice place you have here, Jabez Holmes.
At the center of town but still quiet.
Don't bother, I'll sit on this stone
turtle's back. Moss breaks through the granite
but nothing I do can interrupt your work.
Where is everyone else? We're alone.
Does Francestown liven up after dark?
All I hear is a power saw's moan
at the throat of a pine. The tree holds
its tongue. On the dead air, suddenly a smell
a vital sign rises: manure. The gelded
Morgan tests his barbed wire wall.
And look, Jabez. Empty bottles of Tuborg.
Now, running, two kids with a red dog.

                    *

It must have been hard here. I mean more
than the granite. I mean cold and hungry hard
waiting and praying hard, nothing for the fevers.
Jabez, for instance, with two wives in this sod
before him and thirty years to live out alone.
His Sally, only daughter, stopped at three.
There must have been times when Jabez ran
out of faith and drank too much brandy
or whipped the horses. Times when a watered silk
gown made Sarah, Elizabeth dance in his mind
again. Anniversaries he'd rather not think
about, hand-knitted mufflers he wouldn't find.
Days when Jabez wondered what for
and walked miles over fresh snow, anywhere.

                    *

The clock tower of the Old Meeting House,
gathered 1773, sends four
clear notes to the ruffled sky. Loss
is what I am thinking of. How the shore
recedes, how the headstones these boats
toss in time's groundswell and the names
wear thin. I see Sarah who ballasts the oak
floating out on the 36th year of her age,
Jabez turning his face into the wind.
Eight years later, Elizabeth at 37.
Here, I am old enough to be underground
too, incognito. So are my children.
We did it, you can, sings the chorus.
On 136 West, the logging trucks pass.

The Aga Khan

My Aunt Bibi
Used to visit by surprise
With her husband, Uncle Bob,
A Cadillac convertible and silver
Furs and the thirteen tiny
Carved ivory elephants
Herded into a ring
Given her, she said, by the Aga Khan
Who I imagined rode those elephants
In and out of the ring on her finger.
The summer Bibi lay down
On Mother's bed and moaned
I could see her beauty
Reflected in the mirror
As I stood in the kitchen
Looking in. I saw the scars
Criss-cross
Her shapely back and fanny.
After the doctor
Shot her up, she laughed,
Her eyelids fluttering up and down.
Then she sat in the parlor
Playing gin. Father took me out
For a game of catch,
Muttering *morphine,*
Morphine, son of a bitch.
And when
Two years later I saw my mother
All dolled up at the funeral
Kiss my Uncle Bob, lipstick
Streaking across his cheek,
When I saw the draped casket
And the people milling around
I snuck off to the mens' room
And tried to laugh
Aunt Bibi's laugh, and wondered
What ever happened to the Aga Khan,
That son of a bitch
Who used to ride those elephants
In and out of the ring,
And what a conqueror he must have been,
Her protector, friend,
On his sensuous passage in
And out of that tiny universe
And when would he ever stop?

Gregory Orr

Friday Lunchbreak

At noon, still wearing their white
plastic helmets and long smocks,
they leave the frozen slabs
of calf hanging from aluminum
hooks on the loading docks
and stride down the street
past my window, headed
for the bank on the corner.
I remember the gray calf we found
last spring in Virginia, hidden
by its mother in a gully;
at six days it scampered
and wobbled. We watched
it grow heavy and slow, until
half a year later, fouled
with its own shit and dull of eye,
it stood with the other cattle,
hock deep in muck by the barn.
Then it was gone, perhaps north
to this gallows place, where the men
tromp back, grinning, some with bottles
in brown paper sacks, these men
in spattered white smocks
who are as thick and wide
as the sides of beef they hug
and wrestle, angels of meat.

Robert Pack

The Kiss
> *for Kevin*

A glaze of ice glistens in the manure
and rutted mud of the plowed-under garden
as the brittle crack and squish of my greased boots
leads me plodding beside my vague reflection
this crisp April morning, as if my image
still were in the thawing earth I planted,
and last year's buried spring still stirred and shined
within the slick clay of the chunky soil.

With boot-grooves packed with mud, my cold cleft toes
imagine they can feel the rising moisture;
stopping by a three-year *red delicious* tree
to scrape a fresh bud with my fingernail,
I see that it is green inside -- alive,
having survived the winter in my care.
Yes, it is soft and moist, it has come through
under my care, and I remove the wrapping --
aluminum foil and tape -- around its trunk
that saved it from the gnawing mice and voles
who girdle fruit tree barks beneath the snow.
Now on the yellowed grass, the perfect turds
of starving deer, glimmering like planets,
circle the tree, and the faint waft of skunk
brushes me with a puff of wind; I like it,
it quickens my sense at the exquisite edge
where pleasure cloys, where one knows surely
what the human limits are. I kneel
beside another tree as if to dress
a child for school, snipping a dead branch,
as sharp sun strikes the creased foil by my knee,
catches my dazzled eyes and makes them tear.
A stranger here might think I truly wept.

Spring blood sings in my veins even as it did
some thirty years ago when I planted
my first apple tree. No lessening
of pleasure dulls the sun's feel on my arms,
a warming chill, or the female curves I see
along the hill that fruit trees make when my eyes
follow slowly, caressing every slope,
then moving on. I am gathering my life in
now with a breath, I know what thoughts I must
hold back to let my careful body thrive
as bone by bone it was designed to do.

A gust of wind comes off the upper slope.
Having followed me, my youngest son,

crying "Watch me, Dad!" runs along the ridge
much faster than I thought he could, launching
his huge, black birthday kite; catching the wind,
the kite leaps for the sky, steadies itself
as the string goes taut. It glides above me, swoops,
floating its shadow on my squinting eyes
that, pruning snippers still in hand, I shield
from shocking light. Designed like a great bat—
hooked wings and pointed ears and long white fangs
grinning like Dracula -- it swoops again,
eclipsing the sun, hovers, dives at me;
I see the mock blood oozing at its mouth
and random dribbles brightening its belly
just as it crashes in the apple tree.

I take more shining foil from the tree
and roll it into two enormous teeth,
set them in my mouth like fangs, and chase
my son across the field, running faster
than I thought I could until my ribs
smolder in my chest and my clay hooves ache.
He screams as if the demons of his sleep,
returning from the frozen underground,
were actually upon him -- as I catch him,
grapple him down, sink my gleaming teeth
into his pulsing throat and suck, suck deeper
than I have ever sucked, tasting his life
sweeter than any apple I have known.

Linda Pastan

Ethics

In ethics class so many years ago
our teacher asked this question every fall:
if there were a fire in a museum
which would you save, a Rembrandt painting
or an old woman who hadn't many
years left anyhow? Restless on hard chairs
caring little for pictures or old age
we'd opt one year for life, the next for art
and always half-heartedly. Sometimes
the woman borrowed my grandmother's face
leaving her usual kitchen to wander
some drafty, half imagined museum.
One year, feeling clever, I replied
why not let the woman decide herself?
Linda, the teacher would report, eschews
the burdens of responsibility.
This fall in a real museum I stand
before a real Rembrandt, old woman,
or nearly so, myself. The colors
within this frame are darker than autumn,
darker even than winter -- the browns of earth,
though earth's most radiant elements burn
through the canvas. I know now that woman
and painting and season are almost one
and all beyond saving by children.

Joyce Peseroff

Approaching Absolute Zero

Friends
we are approaching absolute zero
which is a physical concept
which is a concept in physics we have not seen
and if we have seen it
there is no need.
Simply, then,
there is need. When we get to the point
which is a physical concept
when we get to the point of absolute zero
we will be content
to be as we are
the continent of our bodies
now rising now sinking
will be still as the oceans on the moon
rigid as a flag
erect as the physical concept.
Friends
when we enter absolute zero
we will fill its boundaries
we will no longer approach it like the moon
veering into the ocean or the ocean in
to the contentment of the earth.
Still we will come absolutely
to the point of it
and we will feel the point of it
physically
as we need to do
being, as we are,
not content
but under the ocean looking up
like lost continents
or the lost flags of the continents
or the concept of it.

Marge Piercy

Night Fight

Yin and yang, they say,
female and male but the real
division at the roots
of the world's knotty tree
is between those whom trouble
sucks to sleep and those
whom trouble racks awake.

In beds, narrow, double and king,
in matrimonial hammocks, on rugs,
in tents and sleepingbags they lie.
They have just quarreled. The rent
is three months overdue. The roof
leaks blood. The operation looms.
She stares at the ceiling
where demon faces flicker grinning
and he snores.

Suppose anger grips her,
a rat in a terrier's jaws.
How can you sleep?
she roars and he moans
How can you wake me?
groping for the clock.
It's three bloody a.m.!
Rolls over, diving.

He is a pumpkin ripening.
He is a watermelon of sweet
seedy dreams. He is a cask
seething with fermentation.
He bubbles like a hot spring.
He sticks to the sheets like mud.

Divorce or strangulation
are imminent. Those anxiety
stirs hate those anxiety
stills. The conscious
being conscious at four a.m.
cannot forgive.

Robert Pinsky

Tennis
To Howard Wilcox

1. The Service
The nerve to make a high toss and the sense
Of when the ball is there; and then the nerve
To cock your arm back all the way, not rigid

But loose and ready all the way behind
So that the racket nearly or really touches
Your back far down; and all the time to see

The ball, the seams and letters on the ball
As it seems briefly at its highest point
To stop and hover—keeping these in mind,

The swing itself is easy; forgetting cancer,
Or panic learning how to swim or walk,
Forgetting what the score is, names of plants,

And your first piece of ass, you throw the racket
Easily through Brazil, coins, mathematics
And *haute cuisine* to press the ball from over

And a slight slice at two o'clock or less,
Enough to make it loop in accurately
As, like a fish in water flicking itself

Away, your mind takes up the next concern
With the arm, ball, racket still pressing down
And forward and across your obedient body.

II. Forehand
Straightforwardness can be a cruel test,
A kind of stagefright threatening on the cold
And level dais, a time of no excuses.

But think about the word " *stroke*," how it means
What one does to a cat's back, what a brush
Does through a woman's hair. Think about

The racket pressing, wiping, guiding the ball
As you stay on it, dragging say seven strings
Across the ball, the top edge leading off

To give it topspin. Think about the ball
As a loaf of bread, you hitting every slice.
Pull back the racket well behind you, drop it

And lift it, meeting the ball well out in front
At a point even with your left hip, stroking
To follow through cross-court. The tarnished coin

Of "follow through," the cat, the loaf of bread,
"Keep your eye on the ball," the dull alloy
Of homily, simile and coach's lore

As maddening, and as helpful, as the Fool
Or Aesop's *Fables*, the coinage of advice:
This is the metal that is never spent.

III. Backhand

Here, panic may be a problem; in the clench
From back to jaw in manic you may come
Too close and struggling strike out with your arm,

Trying to make the arm do everything,
And failing as the legs and trunk resist.
All of your coinages, and your nerve, may fail...

What you need is the Uroborus, the serpent
Of energy and equilibrium,
Its tail between its jaw, the female circle

Which makes it easy: all is all, the left
Reflects the right, and if you change the grip
To keep your hand and wrist behind the racket

You suddenly find the swing is just the same
As forehand, except you hit it more in front
Because your arm now hangs in front of you

And not behind. You simply change the grip
And with a circular motion from the shoulder,
Hips, ankles, and knees, you sweep the inverted swing.

IV. Strategy

Hit to the weakness. All things being equal
Hit crosscourt rather than down the line, because
If you hit crosscourt back to him, then he

Can only hit back either towards you (crosscourt)
Or parallel to you (down the line), but never
Away from you, the way that you can hit

Away from him if he hits down the line.
Besides, the net is lowest in the middle,
The court itself is longest corner-to-corner,

So that a crosscourt stroke is the most secure,
And that should be your plan, the plan you need
For winning—though only when hitting from the baseline:

From closer up, hit straight ahead, to follow
The ball to net; and from the net hit shrewdly,
To get him into trouble so he will hit

An error, or a cripple you can kill.
If he gets you in trouble, hit a lob,
And make it towering to make it hard

For him to smash from overhead and easy
For you to have the time to range the backcourt,
Bouncing in rhythm like a dog or seal

Ready to catch an object in mid-air
And rocking its head—as with your plan in mind
You arrange yourself to lob it back, and win.

    V. Winning
Call questionable balls his way, not yours;
You lose the point but you have your concentration,
The grail of self-respect. Wear white. Mind losing.

Walk, never run, between points: it will save
Your breath, and hypnotize him, and he may think
That you are tired, until your terrible

Swift sword amazes him. By understanding
Your body, you will conquer your fatigue.
By understanding your desire to win

And all your other desires, you will conquer
Discouragement. And you will conquer distraction
By understanding the world, and all its parts.

Stanley Plumly

Summer Celestial

At dusk I row out to what looks like light or anonymity,
too far from land to be called to, too close to be lost,
and drag oar until I can drift in and out of a circle,
the center of a circle, nothing named, nothing now to see,
the wind up a little and down, building against the air,
and listen to anything at all, bird or wind, or nothing
but the first sounds on the surface, clarifying, clear.

Once, in Canada, I saw a man stand up in his boat and pass
out dollar bills. It was summer dark. They blew down
on the lake like moonlight. Coming out of his hands
they looked like dollar bills. When I look up at the Dippers,
the whole star chart, leaves on a tree, sometimes all night,
I think about his balance over cold water, under stars,
standing in a shoe, the nets all down and gathering.

My mother still wakes crying do I think she's made of money.
—And what makes money make money make money?
I wish I could tell her how to talk herself to sleep.
I wish. She says she's afraid she won't make it back.
As in a prayer, she is more afraid of loneliness than death.
Two pennies for the eyes, two cents: I wish I could tell her
that each day the stars reorganize, each night they come back new.

Outside tonight the waters run to color with the sky.
In the old water dream, you wake up in a boat, drifting out.
Everything is cold and smells of rain. Somewhere back there,
in sleep, you remember weeping. And at this moment you think
you are about to speak. But someone is holding on, hand
over hand, and someone with your voice opening and closing.
In water you think it will always be your face that floats

to the surface. Flesh is on fire under water. The nets go back
to gather and regather, and bring up stones, viridian and silver,
whatever falls. In the story, the three Dutch fishermen sail out
for stars, into the daylight hours, so loaded with their catch
it spills. They sleep, believe it, where they can, and dry
their nets on a full moon. For my mother, who is afraid to sleep,
for anyone afraid of heights or water, all of this is intolerable.

Look, said the wish, into your lover's face. Mine over yours.
In that other life, which I now commend to you, I have spent
the days by a house along the shore, building a boat, tying
the nets together, watching the lights go on and off on the water.
But nothing gets done, none of it ever gets finished. So I lie down
in a dream of money being passed from hand to hand in a long line.
It looks like money—or hands taking hands, being led out

to deeper water. I wake up weeping, and it is almost joy.
I go outside and the sky is sea-blue, the way the earth is looked at
from the moon. And on the great surfaces, water is paying
back water. I know, I know this is a day and the stars reiterate,
return each loss, each witness. And that always in the room next door
someone is coughing all night or a man and a woman make love,
each body buoyed, even blessed, by what the other cannot have.

Rochelle Ratner

A Someday Song For Sophia

Mother, close your eyes.
It seems you've tired.

Were my cradle large
you'd lie beside me.
Hard as I might kick
these sides won't tumble.
My arms can't reach over.

Tiptoe from my room.
This is sharing also.
Put your ear
tightly to the wall.
See, it's still breathing.

Mother, go to bed.
Gracefully, for father needs you.

David Ray

Thanks, Robert Frost

Do you have hope for the future?
Someone asked Robert Frost, toward the end.
Yes, and even for the past, he replied,
that it will turn out to have been all right
for what it was, something we can accept,
mistakes made by the selves we had to be,
not able to be, perhaps, what we wished,
or what looking back half the time it seems
we could so easily have been, or ought . . .
The future, yes, and even for the past,
that it will become something we can bear.
And I too, and my children, so I hope,
will recall as not too heavy the tug
of those albatrosses I sadly placed
upon their tender necks. Hope for the past,
yes, old Frost, your words provide that courage
and it brings strange peace that itself passes
into past, easier to bear because
you said it, rather casually, as snow
went on falling in Vermont years ago.

Borders

As when you wake before dawn,
still dreaming of bodies –
his body, your body,
the babies wet from their journey,
the dead in their frozen tangles.

And because you are half-asleep,
you understand that we are ghosts
in each others' countries, our memories
mirror-images of landscapes
we believed we had charted.

And even what we call home
is a peninsula of shadows,
whose borders always defeat us,
except for those two we cross,
unexpectedly, only once.

Dennis Schmitz

Cutting Out A Dress

Sara's fingers will find the way
before her eyes do
in the river of print-goods daubed

with human figures.
at thirteen she lays out
a world to fit her imagined body
in the attic room held
by its yellow light high in the treetops.
every night she sheds into the outside

animals her childhood taught:
no panda or hippogriff,
but Jake our setter run down by a car,
a snail popped underfoot,
a sluggish fly tapping
out its life between two panes,

each death a kind of rhythmic moulting,
a forgiven pain
her scissors briefly isolates.
in the bedroom below, my wife
& I each think we wrestle
a different angel as we shake

& pant in an unbreakable marriage hold.
the floor above us trembles--
the sewing machine
thumping the same cloth over & over.
the pulse is threaded

into the arm-linked humans
repeated to infinity--
a life so simple its seamless embrace
could be skin itself.

Richard Shelton

Face

you are the mask I was given
and I am what you were given to mask
both of us could have done better
but we had no choice

sometimes late at night
I meet you by accident in the mirror
and you break the silence like a violin
played by a chimpanzee

nothing on your left side
matches anything on your right side
and even if it did you would be
but slightly improved

you go before me
announcing my presence
like a bad omen a harbinger of doom
I keep telling everybody I am
not unhappy it is only my face

and you tell them I am lying
you tell them I am
full of pain and vanity
I am proud and contemptuous
your lips form into a hard line
and you tell them I am growing old
in debauchery

but it is not true
ugly face it is not true

inside me I am
what you could never be
clean featured the eyes are deep-set
and clear the jaw is strong
there is a cleft in the chin
teeth are straight and without gaps

inside me I believe
I have always believed
in a world without freckles
where hair remains faithful to its head
and ears come in matching pairs

Jane Shore

Persian Miniature

With two hairs plucked from the chest of a baby squirrel,
and no lapses of attention,
the brush of the miniaturist freezes an entire population.
Within each quarter-inch surveyed and magnified,
a dozen flowers puncture the spongy ground,
and even the holes where tent-poles stuck
bear ornamental weeds.
Upon a wooden balance beam, this picture's equator,
a cat is prancing.
All the other animals are eating or being milked:
three spotted goats, a beige suede camel,
half a donkey's face lost in an embroidered feedbag.
Under an enormous canopy, seven elders in pajamas radiate
like spokes around the bridegroom.
The whitest beards frost the elders' chins.
Outside, a fat iron cauldron squats upon a fire
whose flames spike up little golden minarets.
A kneeling boy pours coffee;
his pitcher handle's the size of a human eyelash,
but larger than the bridegroom's mustache.
It's a wedding! Is the bride asleep somewhere?
The bride's attendants hover in tiers
like angels in heaven's scaffolding,
but heaven, here, is the hanging gardens,
or maybe the tent-poles hold the heavens up.
Lappets of a tent fold back
on a woman holding her soft triangular breast
to an infant's mouth. The rug she sits on
flaps straight up behind her like wallpaper.
One-sixteenth of an inch away,
a ram is tethered to the picture frame.
But where's the bride going to fit?
In the left hand corner of the painting
across what little of the sky remains,
two geese fly in tandem, pulling two wheels,
two mechanical knotted clouds.
Maybe they are pulling a storm behind them.
Crouched, swirling above the human event,
if the storm fits, it could ruin everything —
smash up the whole abbreviated acre,
flush the bride from sleep —
while the bridegroom sweeps it all away,
entering her innocent tent like thunder
and shatters the distance he's had to keep.

Charles Simic

Butcher Shop

Sometimes walking late at night
I stop before a closed butcher shop.
There is a single light in the store
Like the light in which the convict digs his tunnel.

An apron hangs on the hook:
The blood on it smeared into a map
Of the great continents of blood,
The great rivers and oceans of blood.

There are knives that glitter like altars
In a dark church
Where they bring the cripple and the imbecile
To be healed.

There's a wooden block where bones are broken,
Scraped clean—a river dried to its bed
Where I am fed,
Where deep in the night I hear a voice.

Knute Skinner

The Cow

There's a white cow standing upon the hill,
surely the whitest cow I shall ever see.
As usual with cows she is eating grass.
Nothing strange about that, except that the light,
the white light of the sun increases *her* white
until she seems like a moon reflecting the sun,
a cow-shaped moon newly materialized
to dazzle upon the rise of a grassy hill.
Perhaps she is the cow that jumped over the moon,
but how much grass can she nonchalantly bite
with that white light breaking upon her body?
O, now she raises her head and, striking a pose,
commands the field with a curve of her delicate tail.
And so I see that she has become a goddess
exacting and appreciating the homage
owed to a white spirit by darker creatures.
Those dull cows browsing in brown below her,
mere cows, I see that they cannot comprehend
how their appearance enhances the white goddess.
And yet their heads are lowered in due respect.
She is their deity as she is mine,
although I see her only from my distance.
I see her only through my grimy window.
Suppose I left my papers and left my desk,
walked through the garden, crossed the old stone wall,
slogged through the swamp at the bottom of the hill,
then with lowered eyes I could approach that whiteness.
Would I be touched to some extent by the sunlight,
and would my eyes be blinded with revelation?
Or would I find cowdung beneath my feet,
and would she and I eat grass for the rest of our lives?

Dave Smith

The Perspective and Limits of Snapshots

Aubrey Bodine's crosswater shot of Menchville,
Virginia: a little dream composing a little water,
specifically, the Deep Creek flank of the Warwick.
Two-man oyster scows lie shoulder to shoulder,
as if you walk them, one land to another,
no narrow channel hidden in the glossy middle
like a blurred stroke, current grinning at hulls.
It is an entirely eloquent peace, with lolling
ropes and liquid glitter, this vision of traffic
and no oystermen in sight. Clearly, Bodine is not
Matthew Brady catching the trenchant gropes frozen
at Fredericksburg with a small black box. So well
has he excluded the neat Mennonite church, yachts,
country club pool, the spare smell of dignity seeps.
Perhaps it is because of the zoom on the teeth
of the oyster tongs; perhaps it is after all Sunday.

Above the last boat, the flat-faced store squats
at the end of the dirt road as if musing over
accounts receivable. No doubt it has weathered
years of blood spilling. A spotted hound lifts
his nose above what must be yesterday's trash fish,
his white coat luminous against deep foliage. What
Bodine fails to see is the dog turning to lope
uphill under that screen of poplars, behind fat
azaleas that hide the country farm and the drunks
pressed against wire screens, sniffing the James.
One oysterman thumped his noisy wife (the window
was accidental) because she had a knife and mourned
their boy twenty years drowned. If he knew Bodine
stood at the marsh tip where his boy dove, if he
were but told a camera yawned to suck in the years
of his worst sailing shame, he would turn away. He
would whistle up boys in the dust that is dignity
and if he could he would spit in his hand and tell
his nameless black cellmate there are many men
for whom the world is neither oyster nor pearl.

Six Small Songs For A Silver Flute

1.

I know your secret, now I've caught you
With eyes wide open and lips asleep.

Parts of your body
Nap by turns.

A little finger.
A rib. A breast.

It only seems
You never drowse;

That there's always something
You're ready to tell me.

2.

Each sungold hair
On your forearm wants

Particular love, attended to
Not as amongst all the orphan children

But for herself
— Wants patient lips

To choose *her*, read her
Her bedtime story.

3.

The book in your hand
Explains your life

As best it can.
You're touched. You write it

Friendly notes
In the margins.

4.

A new French blouse . . .
Essentially sleeves.

In it you are
The full flute-theme

Of the sun's
Favorite concerto.

5.

The plastic ferns that smelled so bad
We put them out at the curb, hoping

Someone might steal them
Or bite their clothes off

Are back. They want a second chance.
Should I let them in? They say they've taken

Vows, that in this next life
They'll be wheat.

6.

The more I think
How you walk through the rain

To gather herbs, the thoughtfuller
I get. I know some other songs

But they're all about men, somewhat out of tune,
For kettledrum, and bassoon.

Kathleen Spivack

Approaching the Canvas

She is getting too big. They live in two rooms.
Mother sends her to the Y to learn to paint.
She crayons, she draws pictures labelled "Mother."
She draws the narrow view from her open
window: the sooty roofs of Brooklyn, the sky
smudged. She has trouble focusing

but she tries to keep her life in focus:
the small apartment, the vast dotted rooms
of the museums where each vision of sky
becomes a postage stamp of nature. The paintings
tell her to dare more, to open
her eyes. But she holds on to her mother.

At night in her dreams she calls "Mother"
and her mouth does not move. Only her brain is in focus.
She dreams she is downstairs, opening
a door. She walks into a cellar, through the boiler room
and shoulders her way through a corridor. No sky
here, no light by which to paint

what her blind fingers feel. Cracked paint
pulls her through a narrow hallway. Her mother
recedes into background: the perspective is on sky
pulling her forward; triangular, edging into focus
her blurred dreams. The close room
suffocates. She suffers like birth, hunching toward open

sunlight. The tunnel ends, pushing open
into a technicolor vista like landscape painting
singing, tenderness. Here there is room
for her pomegranate being. Her mother,
black and white, is calling from the background. She focuses
precisely on the present: the cerulean sky,

the sun like petals, the sky
jubilant as her body, opening.
Green fields spread out, like walking into a painting
of her own mind; all her childhood focuses
on this moment, the narrow room
giving way to larger doorways. Even her mother

fades. Flowering, focused, now this girl cries "Mother,"
frightened. She opens herself: there is too much room
in the sky. And she paints a small corner.

William Stafford

Answerers

There are songs too wide for sound. There are quiet
places where something stopped a long time
ago and the days began to open
their mouths toward nothing but the sky. We live
in place of the many who stir only
if we listen, only because the living
live and call out. I am ready
as all of us are who wake at night:
we become rooms for whatever almost
is. It speaks in us, trying. And even if
only by a note like this, we answer.

Alcestis
      for Stanley Kunitz

She pulled her gown from her shoulders,
kicked off her shoes, then passed a mirror:
Her wan face did not appear.
She left without kissing her husband.

In the boat to hell she discovered
that crowded souls flowed together.
She wept at the casual hands
swarming through her heart, waving

away flies or lighting tiny matches
to view the caverns of dark water.
When she smoothed her braid
she could not distinguish it from air.

After the boat docked, she observed
her father on the porch of a hotel
dozing beside the guitar he'd played
at her wedding. She tried to wake him.

Her fingers glided through his jacket.
She could not twang the guitar.
Yet, she thought, a girl once danced
under the stars to its real music.

Would she sleep this sound? Her father
bowed his head, as if listening:
She sensed the eyes at every window
waiting for her to come inside

where a maid turned down the sheets
on the customary mattress of dirt.
At the door she recalled the candles
flaring on her last birthday cake.

What was it she wished for then?
She glanced back across the river
wishing someone called her name.
The stone floor chilled her foot.

The dogs dreaming by the stairs
lifted their muzzles for affection,
but by then she had no gestures left
within her cold and formal hand.

Gerald Stern

In Carpenter's Woods

This is a corner of heaven here,
the moss growing under the leaves,
the rocks cropping up like small graves under the trees,
the old giants rotting in the shade.
I used to come here every Sunday
to stand on the bridge and look at the bird-watchers.
Once I made love in the dead brush
and slept impaled on the thorns, too tired to move;
once I gave myself up to the *New York Times*
and buried myself in sections a whole afternoon;
once I played football with the radicals
while the sun and the rain fought for control.
        At the bottom of the hill where the trees give way to grass
a creek runs through a silent picnic ground
almost a mile away from any access.
Here the neighborhood dogs broke into their runs
at the first threat of authority.
Here the exhibitionists came out in the open
after the long morning with the squirrels and flickers.
Here the Jehovah's Witnesses laid down their arms
and gathered quietly around the tables.
— Without knowing the name or the reason
I gave myself up to vertigo;
I lay for hours with my eyes closed listening to the great sounds
coming in from Germantown;
I loved the ground so much that I had to hold on to the grass for balance.
        I can tell you that where those two girls go carefully over the stones
and where that civilized man and his son
pick up loose wood for the fireplace
was, for three years, my refuge.
I can tell you that I have spent half a lifetime hunting for relief,
that in the simplest locations, in libraries,
in drug stores, in bus stations --
as well as under stone bridges and on hillsides --
I have found places to wait and think.
I tell you that world is as large as the one you sigh and tremble over;
that it is also invulnerable and intricate and pleasurable;
that it has a serious history;
that it was always there, from the beginning.

Mark Strand

Elegy For My Father

(Robert Strand 1908-68)

1 *The Empty Body*

The hands were yours, the arms were yours,
But you were not there.
The eyes were yours, but they were closed and would not open.
The distant sun was there.
The moon poised on the hill's white shoulder was there.
The wind on Bedford Basin was there.
The pale green light of winter was there.
Your mouth was there,
But you were not there.
When somebody spoke, there was no answer.
Clouds came down
And buried the buildings along the water,
And the water was silent.
The gulls stared.
The years, the hours, that would not find you
Turned in the wrists of others.
There was no pain. It had gone.
There were no secrets. There was nothing to say.
The shade scattered its ashes.
The body was yours, but you were not there.
The air shivered against its skin.
The dark leaned into its eyes.
But you were not there.

2 *Answers*

Why did you travel?
Because the house was cold.
Why did you travel?
Because it is what I have always done between sunset and sunrise.
What did you wear?
I wore a blue suit, a white shirt, yellow tie, and yellow socks.
What did you wear?
I wore nothing. A scarf of pain kept me warm.
Who did you sleep with?
I slept with a different woman each night.
Who did you sleep with?
I slept alone. I have always slept alone.
Why did you lie to me?
I always thought I told the truth.
Why did you lie to me?
Because the truth lies like nothing else and I love the truth.
Why are you going?
Because nothing means much to me anymore.
Why are you going?
I don't know. I have never known.

How long shall I wait for you?
Do not wait for me. I am tired and I want to lie down.
Are you tired and do you want to lie down?
Yes, I am tired and I want to lie down.

3 Your Dying

Nothing could stop you.
Not the best day. Not the quiet. Not the ocean rocking.
You went on with your dying.
Not the trees
Under which you walked, not the trees that shaded you.
Not the doctor
Who warned you, the white-haired young doctor who saved you
        once.
You went on with your dying.
Nothing could stop you. Not your son. Not your daughter
Who fed you and made you into a child again.
Not your son who thought you would live forever.
Not the wind that shook your lapels.
Not the stillness that offered itself to your motion.
Not your shoes that grew heavier.
Not your eyes that refused to look ahead.
Nothing could stop you.
You sat in your room and stared at the city
And went on with your dying.
You went to work and let the cold enter your clothes.
You let blood seep into your socks.
Your face turned white.
Your voice cracked in two.
You leaned on your cane.
But nothing could stop you.
Not your friends who gave you advice.
Not your son. Not your daughter who watched you grow small.
Not fatigue that lived in your sighs.
Not your lungs that would fill with water.
Not your sleeves that carried the pain of your arms.
Nothing could stop you.
You went on with your dying.
When you played with children you went on with your dying.
When you sat down to eat,
When you woke up at night, wet with tears, your body sobbing,
You went on with your dying.
Nothing could stop you.
Not the past.
Not the future with its good weather.
Not the view from your window, the view of the graveyard.

Not the city. Not the terrible city with its wooden buildings.
Not defeat. Not success.
You did nothing but go on with your dying.
You put your watch to your ear.
You felt yourself slipping.
You lay on the bed.
You folded your arms over your chest and you dreamed of the
    world without you,
Of the space under the trees,
Of the space in your room,
Of the spaces that would now be empty of you,
And you went on with your dying.
Nothing could stop you.
Not your breathing. Not your life.
Not the life you wanted.
Not the life you had.
Nothing could stop you.

4   Your Shadow

You have your shadow.
The places where you were have given it back.
The hallways and bare lawns of the orphanage have given it
    back.
The Newsboys Home has given it back.
The streets of New York have given it back and so have the
    streets of Montreal.
The rooms in Belém where lizards would snap at mosquitos have
    given it back.
The dark streets of Manaus and the damp streets of Rio have
    given it back.
Mexico City where you wanted to leave it has given it back.
And Halifax where the harbor would wash its hands of you has
    given it back.
You have your shadow.
When you traveled the white wake of your going sent your
    shadow below, but when you arrived it was there to greet you.
    You had your shadow.
The doorways you entered lifted your shadow from you and
    when you went out, gave it back. You had your shadow.
Even when you forgot your shadow, you found it again; it had
    been with you.
Once in the country the shade of a tree covered your shadow and
    you were not known.
Once in the country you thought your shadow had been cast by
    somebody else. Your shadow said nothing.
Your clothes carried your shadow inside; when you took them
    off, it spread like the dark of your past.

And your words that float like leaves in an air that is lost, in a
    place no one knows, gave you back your shadow.
Your friends gave you back your shadow.
Your enemies gave you back your shadow. They said it was
    heavy and would cover your grave.
When you died your shadow slept at the mouth of the furnace
    and ate ashes for bread.
It rejoiced among ruins.
It watched while others slept.
It shone like crystal among the tombs.
It composed itself like air.
It wanted to be like snow on water.
It wanted to be nothing, but that was not possible.
It came to my house.
It sat on my shoulders.
Your shadow is yours. I told it so. I said it was yours.
I have carried it with me too long. I give it back.

5 *Mourning*

They mourn for you.
When you rise at midnight,
And the dew glitters on the stones of your cheeks,
They mourn for you.
They lead you back into the empty house.
They carry the chairs and tables inside.
They sit you down and teach you to breathe.
And your breath burns,
It burns the pine box and the ashes fall like sunlight.
They give you a book and tell you to read.
They listen and their eyes fill with tears.
The women stroke your fingers.
They comb the yellow back into your hair.
They shave the frost from your beard.
They knead your thighs.
They dress you in fine clothes.
They rub your hands to keep them warm.
They feed you. They offer you money.
They get on their knees and beg you not to die.
When you rise at midnight they mourn for you. .
They close their eyes and whisper your name over and over.
But they cannot drag the buried light from your veins.
They cannot reach your dreams.
Old man, there is no way.
Rise and keep rising, it does no good.
They mourn for you the way they can.

6 The New Year

It is winter and the new year.
Nobody knows you.
Away from the stars, from the rain of light,
You lie under the weather of stones.
There is no thread to lead you back.
Your friends doze in the dark
Of pleasure and cannot remember.
Nobody knows you. You are the neighbor of nothing.
You do not see the rain falling and the man walking away,
The soiled wind blowing its ashes across the city.
You do not see the sun dragging the moon like an echo.
You do not see the bruised heart go up in flames,
The skulls of the innocent turn into smoke.
You do not see the scars of plenty, the eyes without light.
It is over. It is winter and the new year.
The meek are hauling their skins into heaven.
The hopeless are suffering the cold with those who have nothing
    to hide.
It is over and nobody knows you.
There is starlight drifting on the black water.
There are stones in the sea no one has seen.
There is a shore and people are waiting.
And nothing comes back.
Because it is over.
Because there is silence instead of a name.
Because it is winter and the new year.

Lucien Stryk

Cherries

Because I sit eating cherries
which I did not pick
a girl goes bad under

the elevator tracks, will
never be whole again.
Because I want the full bag,

grasping, twenty-five children
cry for food. Gorging,
I've none to offer. I want

to care, I mean to, but not
yet, a dozen cherries
rattling at the bottom of my bag.

One by one I lift them to
my mouth, slowly break
their skin -- twelve nations

bleed. Because I love, because
I need cherries, I
cannot help them. My happiness,

bought cheap, must last forever.

Dabney Stuart

The Opposite Field
to my brother

1.

An old photograph shows you
At two or three sitting
In a puddle, mud splattered
On your legs and shirt and face, smiling;
Your arms, having swept through
The water, plunge skyward, filled
                                        I like
To think now
With your delight in simply being there.

There is another from the same period
Of your life showing
You trying to drink from a garden
Hose, the strong skyward arc
Of water thwarting
You, your attention
Immersed, your face
Absolutely composed, without thirst.

In both photographs there is no future.

A figure of someone no less a stranger
Emerges from these two images
The way vapor rises from Aladdin's lamp.
It takes shape, the features of its
Face disposed to suggest your face, your light -
hearted summers mimicked in his gait, the crack
Of the bat, sweet meat, the galling slide
Into second, the earned bruise fading
Into October, the mists of a possible life:

In the form this figure almost achieves
The shadows of your lost seasons call
To each other in the diamond dusk --
Indecipherable voices, echoes,

And I imagine you turning in your bed
Touched vaguely beneath the familiar
Nightmares which have become mere aspects
Of your sleep, touched so far
Back, so close to what you wanted

To be, then, now,
It's as if I said, *Brother,*
Here we are again:

Catch.

2.

June, 1980. You are 39.
Il se situe par rapport au temps:
We will have to follow *that* curve to its end.

3.

I had not thought to find
You so bound,
So driven into the wood.

In the sour locker rooms
We both remember -- stretching
Their dim tunnels from the first
Wet practice all the way
To marriage -- some dog
Would have said, *'Smatter, lost*
Your balls?
        and you would have conned
Him so casually, with such play --
The whole team watching --
He'd have thought you wanted
To borrow his.
        Instead,
In the thick heat of Houston,
On real grass, under a glazed dome
Of sky and no one watching,
You fungo flies to your son,
To me. The thin *tick* of the wood
On the ball rehearses
Itself endlessly, routine
Grounder, routine pop-up, big
Out *tick* routine:

                    after an hour
I take the bat, wave you deep
Down the green reaches, stroking
Them high and long, driving
You to the wall again
And again, up against it time
After time, and then *over*
The wall, Lord, into the next
Field,
        farther,
                    the next season,

Until I don't know where
You are, have never known . . .
                                wanting
Your will and heart to keep
From breaking, impossible,
Your release into the fabulous spaces.

4. *A Lyric Meditation On Sour Locker Rooms*

Almost invariably underground, dank,
At least one corner redolent with urine;
Pasty men, caged, doling; a body count,
One number and another, uniformed, strapped:
Dogsbodies, dog days even in mild April:
                                can you ascend
From this cavern of mock cells, single file,
Into the blare of the green field, virgin again, lined:
                                can you
Remember how to come back down again:
                                and the place
Empty with you in it, alone, benched, cracked
In bone and will, soaked in your own sweat,
The concrete damp under your bare feet, steamed,
And no shower quite able to drown
The echoes of the metal door opening,
Closing,
        the crowd stunned by the high arc
Of the ball hung in the glare, against the dark.

5.

Am I brother to you
The same way I am friend
To the scattered few
People who have woven
Together with me, me
And themselves: I mean, through
Such distance in time
And space that the cloth
Of our love seems to stretch
Into transparency,
The very air of our breath,
Our sightscape, which will catch
Us no matter how far we fall,
And, regardless our sometime will,
Fierce, toward an abrupt end
Of this pantomime,
Will not be riven?
                    Hard
Brotherhood.
                    I prefer the sweet arc
Of the batted ball, grave
And graceful at once, curving
Upward and out, downward and in,
To the enfolding glove.

6.

A newer photograph shows you
And me it's not a game, this life.

The camera arrests neither motion
Nor implicit gesture: you are simply

All there is, you
And the background of stones,

Shadowed -- your face, the lines
In your forehead. Your hair

Recedes. No one needs to tell you

Ghosts share your sleep.

Sometime after the shutter clicks
You probably put on your shirt,

Stand up, and walk
Toward home. The image

Of your possible life
Watches from a distance. Fading,

He picks up a pebble
And tosses it aside, lightly. The sound

Of its landing becomes
Our purest dream.

David Swanger

Rowing In Turns

He
might be plowing
the lake, working
a furrow out into
the full sun,
unmindful
of the anchor
he forgot to pull in,
trailing below
like a heavy hand.

She
opens her legs
against the floorboards
to brace the small
rhythms of her back;
the wake she leaves
is a long apology
for the resistance
of water.

James Tate

Nobody's Business

The telegram arrived
and no one was there to read it.
The hens shooed themselves from the porch,
softly, with tentative pleas for rainwater.
Inside, the house stiffened, halted in mid-flight.
On its nail an apron flapped, then froze.
And in the hallway, slippers fidgeted, then stood
dazed like questionable theatrical props
on the stairs. A suitcase wiped its brow:
so this is the last stop and no one
is here to meet me.

The journey was withdrawn at the last minute:
the footbridge ached now, felt sticky all over.
The station was deserted, and a sweetness like medicine
sculpted the air with numb monosyllables.

Spacious recesses tried imitating a troupe of mimes,
but it was not fair to the exits: they clustered
in a private booth and shakily came to this conclusion:
resources would have to be pooled for the purchase
of a kitten, surely a marginal concession
to the concentration of this new displeasure.

And so, piercing the cold interior, she came
like money into an early morning poker game.
Tousled the shaky ego of the home.
She was the inevitable passenger
who, within days, shriveled into an uncanny submission,
found an alcove in the world and merged
with the unhealthy halting rhythm.

*

A child with his birthday telescope
has observed all this. He tells no one,
it is nobody's business. But nothing is forgotten.
Clad only in fluid intervals, he is untouchable,
mincing toward that housewarming
that is surely his.

Phyllis Thompson

Eurydice

1

There are no trees under the earth.
Good roots go to pulp in the mud.
The rivers of Hell are sludge
Leaking down the red gash
I sank into when I came.

2

I was Eurydice, witness.
The one song Orpheus told was mine.
If the trees attended, if the wind fell gentle to hear,
If thunder over the lightened field withheld,
If the sea hung between tides and did not break,
If lion paced beside fawn and forgot his hunger,
If lovers turned from love's struggle to Orpheus,
It was his tireless telling they overheard.

Earlier than song or lyre
I was ear and listener.
Silence, converse of eyes, was all,
Was need and answer, was mirror, was equal.
A long time breathing quietly.
Breath, the fragrance of other.
The sound in the mind that named the fragrance,
Then correspondent breath, tremor of air,
And in my ear the sound of his thought unwound
The first song of Orpheus.

"Listen."
"I hear."
Heard, in the made hollow,
Himself, musing river,
Wooer and celebrant,
From whom fell the unrefusable music.
For the song, becoming itself, forgot end and origin,
And rose in him without need.
The wind became his motive. The leaves roused.
The trees spread their branches wide to carry his song,
And one bent and became his armed lyre.

Fables of self, streaming in the warm auricle,
Were borne down inner circles, unlaboring,
And burst on the drum
Unchanged,
Pitched purely into the standing air between us,
Heard purely in the purely passive body,

The ear of love.

But when, as he willed, I touched him,
He closed my hands in his hands, stopped the lyre;
He tasted self in my mouth, and the song stopped.

3

In the dry heat of the dog star,
Though the torch of Hymen choked and spit pitch
As it led him to me,
On the other side of the portal
We clasped in our own hands
The truth
Lovelier than every imagined thing,
Harder, happier,
Fact, that perfectly gathers to itself
Light, hymen O hymenaeon,
And Orpheus at peace.
Silent.

As Hell is, till he comes.
As the green world was, till he sang.

4

No serpent killed me.
Nothing that lives would hurt what Orpheus loved.
I walked to the river.
I lay down in the bed.
Something full of us lets go or is torn out
In the warm downpour that floods the declivity,
And we are dead.
In heavy rain I came
Here to Hell.

5

Then to the shaping lyre the trees rose up.
O Orpheus singing! O the tall trees of song!
And all creatures were hushed within themselves
Listening.

6

This way will come Orpheus.
Death will admit him through the soft veins of Hell

For the horned lyre, light lifted among shades.
Within themselves the dead will hear his music, and
A tree will rise in Hell.

Then, like no other,
Singing
Though he eat with the dead,
He will go back
And I will go with him to the portal
Of death's winding ear, where I will listen
As his song reaches into the tender air forever
Living, lucent in the streaming Hebrus, warm
Under the world,
His lyre as stars risen.

John Unterecker

Portrait

If I were to make a portrait, it would be of something fragile:
    a loose suspension of webs,
    grey filaments drifting. . . .

    Already the sky has forgotten evening,
    red saturations folded onto grey light:

       here: nowhere.

Can I tell you the truth?   Ever?

    It is as if I have come in from the garden, my arms full of green promise:
    avocado, papaya, banana, guava, corn, pepper, zucchini --
    yet I can feel only the weight of winter's emptiness against sore muscles.

    When I was a child, I harvested armloads of snow.

We were such liars!

    Heart pulsing in the throat tells no lies:

       the regular lift/fall of taut skin,
       a shadowy rhythm in the hollows of the throat,
       fragile and sure and beautiful:

         Touch me, I change.

So there is an urgency in the way light wrestles with a waking sleeper,
    eyes shifting under sleeping eyelids,
    the parted lips adjusting to dreamed words.

I uncover what I can within half sleep,
    as a ghost might walk an unfamiliar California town keeping almost in step
    or on the deck of a strange ship ask directions of evasive eyes.

Because the wind is out of places I have never been,
    I would hold off dawn,
    red curtains suddenly blown straight out,
    the room brutal with light.

My reach is *under, down, through.*
    Yet I have watched winds lifting out of pine and eucalyptus valleys
    lift to a snowy emptiness where all winds meet.

Far off, on night's other side,
    two surfers ride the slow turn of a breaking wave;
    they steady to its speed—
    a boy and a girl, wet hair swept back through spray,
    mouths open in anticipation of the wave's long ride.

You are a figure on a fold of curving light, swept toward me by the sea,
   hair loose on the pillow, toes testing the slip and drag of the wave:
   a loveliness at the edge of sleep: two figures/ one figure
   pulsing in this single throat.

David Wagoner

Under The Sign Of Moth

Having read and written myself almost to sleep, I stretch
Toward the light and see it
There on the otherwise bare ceiling:
A rust-and-black-winged moth
Motionless over our heads, waiting for something --
The scent of a distant, screened-off mate? Some hint
Of a flower to feed on? Another chrysalis?

My wife is already sleeping, not knowing
We will spread our dreams under the Sign of Moth,
A constellation presiding over us
(More plausibly than the thread-spinning of stars
That housed our births) by clinging
Somehow to the plaster heaven we trusted
To see us safely and vacantly through the night.

I turn out the lamp that might have tempted it
To flutter down and play its familiar role
As a fool for brightness, a hopeful dabbler
Aspiring long enough to expire, battered
And singed by what it thought it wanted,
To suffer a last demeaning transformation
Into a moral lesson.

In the near-darkness, its eyes catch at the streetlight
And gleam deep red, lidlessly staring
Downward at the beginning of our sleep.
What can I offer it but peace and quiet?
With heavy eyelids, I return its gaze
More and more heavily, now blinking, my body
Unable to rise to this occasion,

Either to hunt for love or food or light
Or to fashion a moth-net from some gauzy remnant
Or to manage anything but a spinning fall
Into a dream of becoming
A shape that wants to leave old forms behind,
Now hidden, now crawling upwards, now flying,
Endlessly new, endlessly unfolding.

The ceiling is blank in the morning.
I yawn and slip out from under, obeying the obscure
Scheme of the day, drifting from room to room.
The moth is somewhere in a dusty crevice,
Its long tongue coiled more certainly than a spring
Made to keep time, still waiting
For what it came to find and will die for.

Diane Wakoski

My Mother's Milkman

Cloyce Hamilton,
a slender tan man in white uniform,
with gold teeth,
the truck stopping with foot-clack suddenness
on the gravel road,
the carrier holding 4 glass bottles of whole milk
with their little paper caps crimped over
the tops

My mother in her navy blue wool bathrobe
standing by the blue and white tile
kitchen sink, drinking her first morning cup of coffee

She opens the door for Cloyce
and they stand talking,

For eight years,
three days a week, The Pellisier Dairy Truck
stops with its standing milkman-driver,
Cloyce Hamilton, dressed in white, his tan long wrists and hands
emerging from white starched sleeves,
my mother's King of Spain.

Sometimes my mother ironing in the kitchen
or just drinking coffee.
Waiting to exchange a few words, or
to catch a glimpse of Cloyce Hamilton or
sometimes
to give him a cup of coffee and listen
to the story of his life.

                    She loved to hear
how a man suffered and longed beyond his milkman's life.

My mother and sister and I
visited the Hamiltons sometimes.
Their house was carpeted, dark, and had
a gold-framed oil painting of a California desert scene over
the mantel.
Vera wore her dark hair in a bun, was handsome,
their house smelled like mothballs and
I envied them; they were the typical
average American family.
Handsome father, who drove his milk truck everyday.
Beautiful mother, who had her dining room table polished and a gold-
framed oil over the mantel.
Two plump girls who wore (and how I envied them)

patent leather shoes.

In my early adolescence
I remembered long murmured conversations between my mother
and Cloyce Hamilton, and then one day
she said
we were going to visit Cloyce,
that he was no longer living with Vera and the girls.

We went to a tiny house by the railroad tracks. Inside was handsome Cloyce
and a big teen-aged boy. I don't remember his name. But Cloyce wanted to adopt
the boy, said my mother, and bring him home, and I gathered the whispered conver-
sations had been about his struggles with Vera. How my mother loved to sympa-
thize with men about their struggles with their wives. My poor sad husbandless
mother. The closest she ever came to seduction -- listening to the whispers of
angry or frustrated men, about their own sad faithful wives. Cloyce finally
left wife and daughters to live with this tough, homeless boy.

None of it quite made sense to me.
I questioned and questioned my mother
who was a scorpion-like listener, with her secrets,
dark pools in which undetermined creatures swam.
Now, in retrospect, the story of my mother's milkman
seems still veiled. And sad.
She, such a lonely woman, getting up each morning
for her handsome milkman
who lived the family life she yearned for,
and he, tortured, bent soul
wanting the love of a young boy.

What I remember often is this scene:
            the Hamilton's dark house,
            the gold-framed painting of the California desert
            glowing in the room across from the polished
            dining room table,
            the smell of mothballs,
            the dark Vera, like a Spanish lady,
            and the smell of darkness
            in the house.

My mother believing, to the end,
that Cloyce only wanted a son,
never admitting her handsome milkman
King of Spain,
loved boys.

After all those years of waiting

in the kitchen, at dawn, for the thick milk which she put in her
German coffee.
Drinking.
Fourteen cups a day.
Relieving the black caffeine bitterness
with cream from California's
Pellisier Dairy.

Cary Waterman

Love Poem
      for M.

I. New Jersey, 1959

Morning settles in
through the windows.
We are so young,
two girls as graceful as
the leatherbound books
silently arranged in your father's study.

We read together
following Joyce through
the poorness of Dublin,
Thomas Mann into the family
of *Buddenbrooks.*
And finally Hesse
probing, dissecting
the heart of *Steppenwolf.*

And still we do not suspect a loss,
still we love each other,
growing up together
our vines braided on
the same trellis of light.

Beyond our windows
the seabirds seek from the shore
the long days of summer.
And we turn in this last peace,
sensing the slight blue wind
and our own faithfulness.

And we hear a few miles off
in the Atlantic
the shells turning also
over and over into memory.

II. Minnesota, 1978

Who betrayed us?
And when finally did we
betray each other,
sealing ourselves off
in the rain forest of domestication?

You have gone long ago
across one continent
and one ocean
to live in the shadow of Joyce's tower.
I have come here
where tonight mist rises from
the prairie of Minnesota
and rubs its thumbs against my window.

We have lost each other.
We do not speak of how we are
both encircled by children
as light as floating candles,
of the bondage of small loves growing,
of pain that is as plentiful as grass.

I only hear secondhand
you will have a new baby,
and that you keep honey bees
near your old stone house.
And that you are thin,
thin, and smoke too much,
striking match on match for fire.

Theodore Weiss

En Route
for Harry and Kathleen

Things we, sinking
in an anytime mid-darkness,
cling to which might get us
out of this mess or at least
bring it into focus — no wonder
they grow wonderful,
                          perched
five stories up in this study
of a spacious New York apartment,
the rooms, every one, cosily lined
with ceiling-high shelves, books
behind books, art-books, recordings,
pictures like the cave at Lascaux,

the mousy little cat, a thing
of springs, projected across
the room, the other, furtive,
prickly, humped on topmost volumes,

a grey enough day, the day
before Christmas, at the Riverside,
buses soughing by, the buildings,
that glittered Byzantine last night
like Christmas itself, this morning
bulky cut-outs made of mist,
risen from the river,
                          sitting
at my friend's desk, drawers
no doubt littered with postcards,
letters, bills like crumpled sails
of voyages forgotten, our trip
to the Far East fast approaching,

he sightseeing with Kathleen
in Rome or this very moment maybe
floating along, as in my revery,
on a gondola in Venice, its waves
blown, a Byzantine, into shapes
mercurial as their colors,

                              I
clinging to things not my own,
this bottle of glue, stuck fast
to itself, that jar of pencils,
the typewriter with its tier
on tier of a population waiting —
then it boos, it cheers — to be
manipulated,
                    able to compose
who knows what lightning
phrases, able at once to stab
us into wounds we'd rather keep
covered
              and to soothe them
with recovering balm of something
discovered, something almost
understood.

                    Through the plants
stacked on the ledge I squint
out the window, hoping the day,
like glue in the bottle, will hold
at least itself together

                              and say
that it, no less than the phone
reposed on the desk, contains
assorted messages can find me
out in an instant, targeted
as by a scream or cat-quick music,
with homesick grief, everywhere
fondling, homecome laughter.

                              Oh
must disconsolateness, this feeling
unmade up like a many-times-slept-
in bed, this clutter, leaves
scuffed, grounded, several times
faded, bitter grey everywhere,
fit and fit and fit me?

Richard Wilbur

Transit

A woman I have never seen before
Steps from the darkness of her town-house door
At just that crux of time when she is made
So beautiful that she or time must fade.

What use to claim that as she tugs her gloves
A phantom heraldry of all the loves
Blares from the lintel? That the staggered sun
Forgets, in his confusion, how to run?

Still, nothing changes as her perfect feet
Click down the walk that issues in the street,
Leaving the stations of her body there
As a whip maps the countries of the air.

Charles Wright

Called Back

Friday arrives with all its attendant ecstacies.
Mirrors bloom in the hushed beds.

The ocotillo starts to extend
                    its orange tongues
Down in Sonora, the cactus puts on its beads.
Juan Quesada's Angel of Death, socket and marrow bone,
Stares from its cage and scorched eyes.

I've made my overtures to the Black Dog, and backed off.
I've touched the links in its gold chain.
I've called out and bent down and even acknowledged my own face.

Darkness, O Father of Charity, lay on your hands.

For over an hour the joy of the mockingbird has altered the leaves.
Stealthily, blossoms have settled along the bougainvillaea like
                                                purple moths
Catching their breaths, the sky still warm to the touch.
Nothing descends like snow or stiff wings
Out of the night.
                    Only the dew falls, soft as the footsteps of the
                                                        dead.

Language can do just so much,
                    a flurry of prayers,
A chatter of glass beside the road's edge,
Flash and a half-glint as the headlights pass . . .

When the oak tree and the Easter grass have taken my body,
I'll start to count out my days, beginning at 1.

Paul Zweig

A Fly On The Water

I

It is eating me,
Working its way into me like breath.
It is everything hungry in the world,
And wants me, and I'll tell you, I don't mind.
The women I meet are soft fire,
And at night,
When colors drain from the solid world,
I hear space rattling in my heart;
Your voice,
That muffled angry breathing.

My fathers shuffle the sky,
Smelling of pine trees, dark sandy soil.
The individual breaks the chain. I am lonely,
And think of those sad mystical men in their dark hats,
Who made God's noise when they prayed,
Made it louder in their goosedown beds,
When they clapped their wives' ears,
And heard God's drum
Measuring their bones, and their skin, and blood.

II

A child is stretching his arms out
In the summer heat. With eyes half closed,
He feels the life spilling inside him.
Small and pale on the grass,
He looks almost cruel, he is so happy.

The tree shakes, and God falls out.
Lifetimes of skin and longing
Stroll naked in the street.
I do this because it is all I know:
My text, a joke of the flesh,
Like eyesight, hummingbirds,
Anything else that soars.

III

Stillness spreads from your face
Like ice knitting a pond edge.
When it breaks, will God stream past my ankle
Darkly, as the mystics see him,
Or as a pool of deadly light
From which life shields me?

A fly skates on nothing, on tension:
Something abstract as a prayer, or as love.

CONTRIBUTOR NOTES

The following format includes each poet's current place of residence, any college, university, or workshop where he or she may teach, and the title of his or her most recent book.

Ai: Miller Place, NY. The Writer's Community, N.Y.C. The Killing Floor (Houghton Mifflin, 1978).

A.R. Ammons: Ithaca, NY. Cornell University. Selected Longer Poems (W.W. Norton, 1980).

Philip Appleman: New York City. Indiana University. Open Doorways (W.W. Norton, 1976).

Amiri Baraka: Newark, NJ. SUNY at Stony Brook. Selected Poetry (Wm. Morrow & Co., 1979).

Marvin Bell: Iowa City, IA. University of Iowa. These Green-Going-To-Yellow (Atheneum, 1981).

Suzanne E. Berger: Somerville, MA. These Rooms (Penmaen Press, 1979).

Robert Bly: La Porte, MN. News of the Universe: Poems of Two Fold Consciousness (Sierra Club, 1980).

Philip Booth: Castine, ME. Syracuse University. Before Sleep (Viking/Penguin, 1980).

Olga Broumas: Plainfield, VT. Goddard College. Soie Sauvage (Copper Canyon Press, 1979).

Charles Bukowski: Los Angeles, CA. Women (Black Sparrow, 1979). .

Hayden Carruth: Syracuse, NY. Syracuse University. Brothers, I Loved You All (Sheep Meadow, 1979).

Ray Carver: Syracuse, NY. Syracuse University. What We Talk About When We Talk About Love (Knopf, 1981).

Philip Dacey: Cottonwood, MN. Southwest State U., Marshall, MN. Men At Table (Chowder Chapbooks, 1980).

Madeline DeFrees: Amherst, MA. University of Massachusetts. When Sky Lets Go (Braziller, 1980).

Stephen Dobyns: Searsport, ME. Boston University, Goddard College. Heat Death (Atheneum, 1980).

Norman Dubie: Tempe, AZ. Arizona State University. The Everlastings (Doubleday, 1980).

Richard Eberhart: Hanover, NH. Dartmouth, University of Florida in Gainesville. Ways Of Light (Oxford University Press, 1980).

Russell Edson: Stamford, CT. With Sincerest Regrets (Burning Deck, 1980).

Alan Feldman: Framingham, MA. Framingham State College. Frank O'Hara (G.K. Hall, 1979).

Carolyn Forché: Barboursville, VA. University of Virginia, Charlottesville. Gathering The Tribes (Yale University Press, 1976).

Tess Gallagher: Syracuse, NY. Syracuse University. Under Stars (Graywolf Press, 1978).

Brendan Galvin: Truro, MA. Central Connecticut State College. Atlantic Flyway (University of Georgia Press, 1980).

Gary Gildner: Des Moines, IA. The Runner (University of Pittsburgh, 1978).

Louise Glück: Plainfield, VT. Goddard College. Descending Figure (Ecco, 1980).

Linda Gregg: Leverett, MA. Too Bright To See (Graywolf, 1980).

Marilyn Hacker: New York City. Columbia University. Taking Notice (Knopf, 1980).

John Haines: Fairbanks, AK. In A Dusty Light (Graywolf, 1977).

Donald Hall: Danbury, NH. Ox Cart Man (Viking Press, 1979).

Mark Halperin: Ellensburg, WA. Central Washington University. Gomer (Sea Pen Press, 1980).

Daniel Halpern: New York City. Life Among Others (Penguin, 1978).

Robert Hass: Berkeley, CA. Praise (Ecco, 1979).

William Heyen: Brockport, NY. SUNY at Brockport. Long Island Light: Poems and a Memoir (Vanguard Press, 1979).

Jim Heynen: Port Townsend, WA. The Man Who Kept Cigars In His Cap (Graywolf, 1979).

George Hitchcock: Santa Cruz, CA. Mirror On Horseback (Cloud Marauder Press, 1979).

Daniel Hoffman: Swarthmore, PA. University of Pennsylvania. Brotherly Love (Random House, 1981).

Richard Hugo: Missoula, MT. University of Montana. The Right Madness on Skye (W.W. Norton, 1980).

David Ignatow: East Hampton, NY. York College. Tread The Dark (Atlantic, Little Brown, 1978).

Laura Jensen: Tacoma, WA. The Story Makes Them Whole (Porch, 1979).

Don Johnson: Bridgewater, MA. Bridgewater State College.

Donald Justice: Iowa City, IA. University of Iowa. Selected Poems (Atheneum, 1979).

X.J. Kennedy: Bedford, MA. The Tigers Of Wrath (University of Georgia Press, 1981).

Faye Kicknosway: Bloomfield Hills, MI. Nothing Wakes Her (Oyster Press, 1978).

Peter Klappert: Alexandria, VA. George Mason University. The Idiot Princess of The Last Dynasty: The Apocryphal Monologues of Doctor Matthew O'Connor (Knopf, 1981).

Bill Knott: Port Townsend, WA. Selected and Collected Poems (Sun, 1977).

Maxine Kumin: Warner, NH. To Make A Prairie: Essays on Poets, Poetry, & Country Living (University of Michigan Press, 1980).

Philip Levine: Fresno, CA. Cal. State U. Seven Years (Atheneum, 1981).

Larry Levis: Columbia, MO. University of Iowa. The After Life (University of Iowa Press, 1977).

Laurence Lieberman: Urbana, IL. University of Illinois. God's Measurements (Macmillan, 1980).

Thomas Lux: New York City. Sarah Lawrence, Goddard College. Sunday (Houghton Mifflin, 1979).

William Matthews: Seattle, WA. University of Washington. Rising and Falling (Atlantic, Little Brown, 1979).

Mekeel McBride: Rochester, NH. University of New Hampshire. No Ordinary World (Carnegie-Mellon, 1979).

Heather McHugh: Eastport, ME. SUNY, Binghamton, Goddard College. Dangers (Houghton Mifflin, 1977).

Sandra McPherson: Portland, OR. University of California, Berkeley. The Year Of Our Birth (Ecco, 1978).

William Meredith: Washington, D.C. Earthwalk: New and Selected Poems (Knopf, 1976).

James Merrill: Stonington, CT. Scripts For The Pageant (Atheneum, 1980).

W.S. Merwin: Maui, Hawaii. Selected Translations 1968-1978 (Atheneum, 1979).

Robert Morgan: Freeville, NY. Cornell University. Groundwork (Gnomon, 1979).

Howard Moss: New York City. Columbia University. Notes From The Castle (Atheneum, 1979).

Lisel Mueller: Lake Forest, IL. Goddard College. The Need To Hold Still (Louisiana State University Press, 1980).

Carol Muske: New York City. Columbia University. Skylight (Doubleday, 1980).

Jack Myers: Dallas, TX. Southern Methodist University. The Family War (L'Epervier Press, 1977).

Howard Nemerov. St. Louis, MO. Washington University. Sentences (University of Chicago Press, 1980).

John Frederick Nims: Chicago, IL. University of Illinois. Sappho to Valery: Poems In Translation (Princeton University Press, 1980).

Carole Oles: Newton, MA. The Loneliness Factor (U. of Texas Tech Press, 1979).

Steve Orlen. Tucson, AZ. University of Arizona. Permission To Speak (Wesleyan University Press, 1979).

Gregory Orr: Earlysville, VA. University of Virginia. The Red House (Harper & Row, 1980).

Robert Pack: Cornwall, VT. Middlebury College. Waking To My Name: New & Selected Poems (Johns Hopkins Press, 1980).

Linda Pastan: Potomac, MD. The 5 Stages of Grief (W.W. Norton, 1978).

Joyce Peseroff: Lexington, MA. The Hardness Scale (Alice James, 1977).

Marge Piercy: Wellfleet, MA. The Moon Is Always Female (Knopf, 1980).

Robert Pinsky: Berkeley, CA. University of California, Berkeley. An Explanation Of America (Princeton University Press, 1979).

Stanley Plumly: Houston, TX. University of Houston. Out-Of-The-Body-Travel (Ecco, 1978).

Rochelle Ratner: New York City. Combing The Waves (Hanging Loose, 1979).

David Ray: Kansas City, MO. University of Missouri. The Tramp's Cup (Chariton Review Press, 1978).

Mariève Rugo: Newton Center, MA.

Dennis Schmitz: Sacramento, CA. California State University. String (Ecco, 1980).

Richard Shelton: Tucson, AZ. University of Arizona. The Bus To Vera Cruz (University of Pittsburgh Press, 1978).

Jane Shore: Seattle, WA. University of Washington. Eye Level (University of Massachusetts Press, 1977).

Charles Simic: Strafford, NH. University of New Hampshire. Classic Ballroom Dances (Braziller, 1980).

Knute Skinner: Bellingham, WA. The Flame Room (Anthelion, 1979).

Dave Smith: Binghamton, NY. SUNY Binghamton. Goshawk, Antelope (University of Illinois Press, 1979).

Barry Spacks: Cambridge, MA. M.I.T. U. of Kentucky. Imagining A Unicorn (University of Georgia Press, 1978).

Kathleen Spivack: Watertown, MA. The Advanced Writing Workshop, Cambridge, MA. Summer In The Spreading Dawn (Applewood Press, 1981).

William Stafford: Lake Oswego, OR. Things That Happen Where There Aren't Any People (Boa Editions, 1980).

Maura Stanton: Eureka, CA. Molly Companion (Bobbs, Merrill, 1977).

Gerald Stern: Raubsville, PA. Somerset County College. Lucky Life (Houghton Mifflin, 1977).

Mark Strand: New York City. Harvard University. The Monument (Ecco, 1979).

Lucien Stryk: DeKalb, Illinois. Northern Illinois University. Encounter With Zen: Writings On Poetry & Zen. (Swallow Press, 1980).

Dabney Stuart: Charlottesville, VA. Washington & Lee University. Round And Round (Louisiana State University Press, 1977).

David Swanger: Santa Cruz, CA. U. of California, Santa Cruz. The Shape Of Waters (Ithaca House, 1978).

James Tate: Pelham, MA. University of Massachusetts. Riven Doggeries (Ecco, 1979).

Phyllis Thompson: Honolulu, HI. University of Hawaii. What The Land Gave (Quarterly Review of Literature, 1981).

John Unterecker: Honolulu, HI. Stone (University Press of Hawaii, 1977).

David Wagoner: Seattle, WA. University of Washington. In Broken Country (Atlantic- Little, Brown, 1979).

Diane Wakoski: East Lansing, MI. Michigan State University. Cap Of Darkness (Black Sparrow, 1980).

Cary Waterman: Le Center, MN.ı Mankato State University. The Salamander Migration (University of Pittsburgh Press, 1980).

Theodore Weiss: Princeton, NJ. Princeton University. Views and Spectacles: New and Selected Shorter Poems (Macmillan, 1979).

Richard Wilbur: Cummington, MA. The Mind Reader and Other Poems (1980).

Charles Wright: Laguna Beach, CA. University of California, Irvine. China Trace (Wesleyan University Press, 1977).

Paul Zweig: New York City. Queens College. Three Journeys: an Automythology (Basic Books, 1976).